The Teacher'S
the Tonic Sol-ʄu ᴀᴢ~

A Guide to the Teaching of Singing in
Schools by the Tonic Sol-Fa System

Alexander T. Cringan

Alpha Editions

This Edition Published in 2020

ISBN: 9789354219580

Design and Setting By
Alpha Editions
www.alphaedis.com
Email – info@alphaedis.com

PREFACE.

THE importance of the study of Music is now freely recognized, and in numerous Towns and Cities it is placed, as a regular subject, upon the curriculum. Progressive teachers throughout the Dominion are now fully alive to the beneficial effects of the study of Music as a refining, moral influence in the schoolroom and the home. Many teachers are earnestly investigating the various "systems" of teaching music, and the majority of those have decided in favor of the Tonic Sol-fa System as being based on true philosophical principles of teaching such as are now employed in teaching all other subjects. This system is not, as many suppose, a new system, having been before the public for upwards of forty years. In England, it has had to contend with most fierce and prejudiced opposition. which it has gradually overcome by its intrinsic merit, until now it is approved by the leading Musicians and Educators, and is used in ninety per cent. of the schools which succeed in passing the Government Examination in Music. In Canada, it has met with the same opposition and suspicion, but as its merits as a system have become known, this has gradually been disarmed, until now it has been adopted by the Educational authorities of the leading Cities and Towns cf the Dominion.

Improved teaching can only be looked for through an improved knowledge of the subject, and increased skill in the methods of teaching by the reguiar teachers. The object of this work is to aid the teacher in presenting the subject in a manner which will make the study a source of pleasure and profit to teac er and pupil alike. The author offers his experience in the hope that it may lighten the labours of his co-workers in a great and good cause.

The plan of this work deals in detail with each branch of the subject, and explains, by means of Specimen Lessons and appropriate suggestions, the simplest and most practical methods of application. A number of exercises are given in each department, which, although insufficient in themselves, will enable the teacher to prepare others as may be deemed necessary

ALEX. T. CRINGAN.

INDEX.

———

MANUAL SIGNS OF TONES IN KEY.

As seen from the left of the teacher, not as seen from the front. Teachers should particularly notice this.

SOH.
The GRAND or *bright* tone.

TE.
The PIERCING or *sensitive* tone.

FAH.
The DESOLATE or *awe-inspiring* tone.

LAH.
The SAD or *weeping* tone.

ME.
The STEADY or *calm* tone.

DOH.
The STRONG or *firm* tone.

RAY.
The ROUSING or *hopeful* tone.

NOTE.—"These proximate verbal descriptions of mental effect are only true of the tones of the scale when sung slowly - when the ear is filled with the key, and when the effect is not modified by harmony."

As seen from the Teacher's point of view, the back of the hand being shown to the pupils.

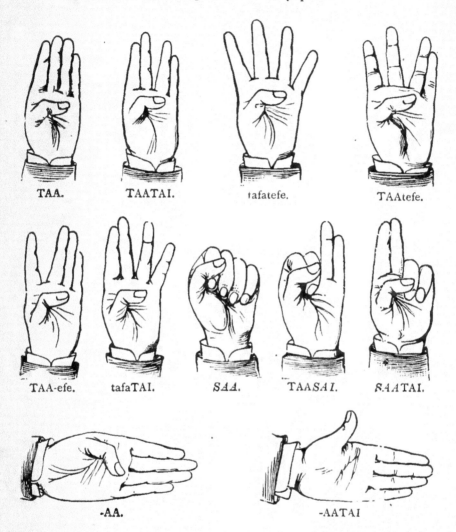

TAA.   TAATAI.   ÷afatefe.   TAAtefe.

TAA-efe.   tafaTAI.   SAA.   TAASAI.   SAATAI.

-AA.   -AATAI

NOTE.—"These Signs are generally given with the left hand to distinguish them from the Hand-signs, which are given with the right. The back of the hand is toward the pupils, so that the thumb may not be seen, for we never divide the pulse into five equal parts. Some Teachers find a difficulty in dividing and joining their fingers quickly enough. To them it will be of great assistance to use the fingers of the right hand inside the held-up left hand, for the purpose of placing and keeping the left-hand fingers as they would wish. Teachers reserve their right-hand for beating time; sometimes tapping the pulses on the top of the left-hand (which is held still), and sometimes beating time in the regular way close by. The wood-cuts are from the Teacher's point of view, not from the side seen by the pupils."

TONIC SOL-FA TIME CHART.

BY JOHN CURWEN.

WHOLES. HALVES.	QUARTERS.	THIRDS.
:1	:1 .1 .1 .1	:1 .1 .1
TAA	tafatefe	taataitee.
:—	:1 .1 ,1	:1 — .1
-AA	TAAtefe	taa-aitee
:	:1 ,1	:1 .1 —
SAA	TAA-fe	taatai-ee
:1 .1	:1 ,1 .1	: .1 .1
TAATAI	tafaTAI	saataitee
:— .1	: ,1 .1 ,1	:1 — ,
-AATAI	safatefe	taa-aisee
: .1	:1 ,1 .1 ,	:1 , ,
SAATAI	tafatese	taasai-ee
:1 .	:1 . ,1	:1 , .1
TAASAI	TAAsefe	taasaitee

EIGHTHS.

:1 1 ,1 1 .1 1 ,1 1

tanafanatenefene

NINTHS.

:1 ¹ 1 ³ ,1 1 1 ³ ,1 1 1

taralatereletirili

SIXTHS (THREE ACCENTS)

:1 1 ,1 1 ,1 1

tafatefetifi

SIXTHS (Two ACCENTS).

:1 ¹ 1 1 ³ .1 1 1

taralaterele

[NOTE.—"Ai" is pronounced as in maid, fail, etc. "Aa" is pronounced as in father, "a" as in mad, "e" as in led, and "i" as in lid. These time-names are copied from M. Paris's "Langue des durées." The minute divisions are seldom used except in Instrumental Music].

HOW TO TEACH

THE

TONIC SOL-FA SYSTEM OF MUSIC.

PART FIRST.

CHAPTER I.

THE STEPS OF THE SYSTEM.

SINCE the introduction of the Tonic Sol-fa system, many teachers have adopted the *notation*, but have not taken sufficient pains to inform themselves of the grading of the various steps, or the methods of presentation which are peculiar to the *system*. As a natural consequence, their teaching has been of an irregular and haphazard description, which has too often, though unintentionally, been the means of bringing discredit on the system. "The easy before the difficult," "the simple before the compound," and "one thing at a time," are maxims with which every teacher is familiar, but their application to the teaching of music is still far from having become general.

The Tonic Sol-fa system is based on the true principles of teaching, and the methods by which they are applied cannot fail to commend themselves to all practical teachers. In order to secure the best possible results, a careful adherence to the steps of the method is absolutely necessary.

The system is divided into six steps. The two principal subjects, *Time* and *Tune*, are taught separately throughout. The arrangement of the primary steps is as follows :—

FIRST STEP.

TUNE.—The **DOH** chord (d m s) with all octaves.

TIME.—Whole pulse tones, half pulse tones and prolonged tones, in two, three or four-pulse measure.

SECOND STEP.

TUNE.—The **SOH** chord (s t r¹) with all octaves.

TIME.—Quarter pulse tones, pulse-and-half tones and silent pulses, in any measure.

THIRD STEP.

TUNE.—The **FAH** chord (f l d¹) with all octaves.

TIME.—Combinations of half and quarter pulse tones, and silent half-pulses.

CHAPTER II.

GENERAL HINTS.

BEGINNING TO TEACH. MANY excellent teachers have been deterred from attempting to teach music by the erroneous impression that only those who are naturally gifted with a good voice or a musical temperament are qualified to teach music. Such, however, is fortunately far from being the case. On the contrary, teachers who are not so gifted, have a much better appreciation of the difficulties to be overcome by their pupils in learning to sing, and can more readily lend assistance when necessary, than the more gifted teachers, who find no serious obstacles in their personal studies of music. Let the teacher, once master the first step and give the first lesson, and difficulties which formerly seemed insurmountable will gradually vanish, to be succeeded by wonder that a subject so full of pleasure and interest to teacher and pupils should have been so long neglected. "We learn to do by doing." Let the teacher keep this fact in mind and act upon it. Whenever a step has been mastered, let it be taught to a class, and confidence in teaching will soon follow. No one refrains from teaching drawing, saying, "I am not an artist," or from teaching reading, because he cannot claim to be an elocutionist, neither should any be deterred from teaching singing because he is not a musician.

QUALITY OF TONE. + Starter Exercise

| SING SOFTLY. | All exercises should be sung with a soft, *pure* tone of voice, and the ten- |

dency to anything approaching loud or harsh singing should be nipped in the bud. A soft pattern should be given by the teacher, and pupils encouraged to imitate it. Every music lesson should be commenced with exercises, in developing a good tone of voice This will be found to exert a beneficial influence throughout the entire lesson. See chapter on voice training. P 169, 125, 132

BEST POSITION FOR SINGING.

This is undoubtedly standing erect, with the head

well kept up, but not thrown back, and the arms hanging easily by the sides. This is not always conveniently attainable, owing to the construction of school desks, or nar-rowness of the aisles. The next best position is sitting erect with the hands hanging easily by the sides, or folded loosely and resting on the desks. The weight of the body must not be thrown on the hands while in the latter position. "Arms folded," or "hands behind," should be avoided, as both tend to obstruct freedom of action of the organs of respiration, which is absolutely indispensable during singing.

> SIT EASILY.

> AVOID "HANDS BEHIND."

SINGING WITH PUPILS.

There is always a strong tendency to sing with pupils whenever the slightest difficulty occurs, but this ought not to be indulged. Pupils may be "pulled through" in this manner, but the exercise will fail to be of the slightest educational value. No sensible teacher would, for a moment, attempt to teach a child to read by simply repeating the lesson with him. In teaching singing, the same laws should be observed as in teaching reading. The teacher should listen, until help is required, then sing while the pupil becomes the listener.

> DO NOT SING WITH PUPILS.

LEARNING BY IMITATION.

This is one of the most important features of the Tonic Sol-fa system. Theory and notation are kept in the back-ground as much as possible, while the *thing*, music, is studied from a pattern given

AVOID BAD PATTERN.

by the teacher. Pupils will readily imitate whether the pattern be good or bad. Teachers should be careful to avoid defective patterning, and should practise in private until sufficient control of voice has been obtained, to secure correctness in intonation and quality of tone in patterning exercises and phrases.

DIVISION OF LESSON.

It is impossible to lay down any definite rule regarding length or frequency of lessons. In this matter circumstances must decide what is most advisable. The plan of devoting all the available time to a single weekly lesson is not calculated to produce the best results. The lessons are too long to permit of the interest being kept awake, and the length of interval between lessons entails a strain on the minds of the pupils to remember what has been taught. Where it is possible, a short lesson should be given daily, but when this cannot be done an effort should be made to have the music lesson at least every alternate day. From twenty to thirty minutes daily is the average time that can be spared for music in the public schools. In order to make the most of the time, the lesson should be planned in advance and a specific time allotted to each subject. The following time-table has been put to a·practical test and found to work satisfactorily :—

Voice-training,	3 minutes.
Modulator drill -	5 "
Sight-singing, -	3 "
Time, -	7 "
Ear-training, -	4 "
Practice of pieces,	8 "

30 minutes.

CHAPTER III.

THE FUNDAMENTAL PRINCIPLES OF THE TONIC SOL-FA SYSTEM.

MUSIC is broadly divided into two branches, viz.: *Tune* and *Time*. Each subject is taught separately, in accordance with the true principle of teaching "one thing at a time."

TUNE.

THE KEY TONE.   All tones are studied in their relation to a governing tone or key-tone called the Tonic, irrespective of their position in the scale of abs·ute pitch. Each tone of the scale has a distinct character or mental effect by which it can be recognized in any key. The appreciation of mental

MENTAL EFFECT.   effect is the most powerful aid to a clear conception of the tones of the scale, without which it is impossible to sing in tune,

When a true conception of the mental effect of tones has been formed, the singer is enabled to sing with a degree of definiteness and accuracy, not easily obtained by any method of what is commonly termed "singing by interval."

MENTAL EFFECTS. (MAJOR MODE.)

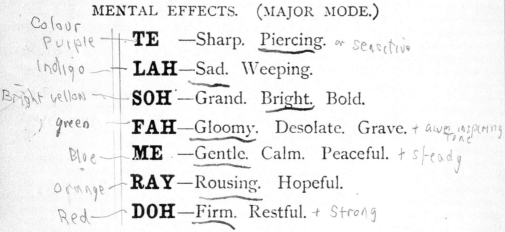

Colour

TE —Sharp. Piercing. *or sensitive* *(Purple)*

LAH—Sad. Weeping. *(Indigo)*

SOH—Grand. Bright. Bold. *(Bright yellow)*

FAH—Gloomy. Desolate. Grave. *+ awe inspiring tone* *(green)*

ME —Gentle. Calm. Peaceful. *+ steady* *(Blue)*

RAY —Rousing. Hopeful. *(Orange)*

DOH—Firm. Restful. *+ Strong* *(Red)*

These approximate descriptions of mental effect are only true of the tones of the scale when sung slowly ; when the ear is filled with the key ; and when the effect is not modified by harmony.

MANUAL SIGNS.

A set of manual signs have been devised which enables the teacher to face the class while giving an indication of the tones desired to be sung. By comparing the diagram of manual signs (page 6), it will be seen that each sign gives a suggestive picture of the mental effect of the tone which it represents. They have been found invaluable as a means of concentrating attention in teaching time ; and so strong is their mnemonic power, that pupils will often

For info on colour choice see P 96-7 and use,

sing, by their aid, difficult intervals, when other means have failed. It must be observed, however, that they are simply a means to an end, and the error of using them to the exclusion of the modulator and blackboard must be avoided.

The major scale is treated as being the same in all keys, and has but one representation for one thing,

> ONE SCALE.

viz. : the initial letters of each note. The following example is written in the key of C, but should it be desired in the key of E, all that is necessary is to substitute E for C and change the pitch of the key-tone ; the notation will remain unchanged :—

KEY C.

|d :m |f :m.r|d :t₁ |d :— ||

KEY E.

|d :m |f :m.r|d :t₁ |d :— ||

The tones are introduced chordally, not diatonically.

> CHORDAL TREATMENT.

This is the method which best accords with the harmony of nature. Tones are more easily sung when arranged chordally, i. e., in groups composed of a tone with its third and fifth, (d m s) (f l d¹) (s t r¹) and by this means pupils are trained to sing wide intervals from the outset. The practice of singing intervals stepwise only is productive of uncertainty in reading at sight, and is narrowing in its effect. The principle of tuning instruments by chord has been followed by musicians for centuries, and recognized as the only true means of securing perfection in tuning; but John Curwen, the founder of the Tonic Sol-fa system, was the first to make a practical application of the principle to the teaching of vocal music.

The tonic chord (**d m s**), the most common chord in music, is composed of the strongest tones of the scale, consequently is the first in order of introduction.

TIME.

Time is taught apart from *Tune*, the exercises in time only being sung on a monotone.

The successful teaching of time depends largely on the recognition of three great facts, viz. :

The existence of pulses in music.

The regularity of pulses.

The accent of pulses and consequent grouping into measures.

EXISTENCE OF PULSES. If pupils be requested to clap hands while a lively tune is being sung, it will be observed that their beats will be almost exactly alike, and will seem to fit into some element of the tune. This element is termed the *pulse* of the tune.

REGULARITY OF PULSES. In any one tune, these pulses will be found to be regular in recurrence and duration, although in some tunes they move faster than in others.

ACCENT AND MEASURE. As in poetry, the accents are of various degrees of strength, so also in music. The regular recurrence of the strong pulse divides the music into measures. When every alternate pulse is strong, there will be two pulses in each measure, and when the strong pulse is followed by two weak pulses, there will be three pulses in each measure.

EXAMPLE :—

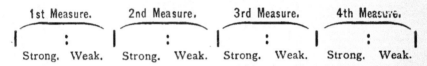

TWO-PULSE MEASURE.

1st Measure.	2nd Measure.	3rd Measure.	4th Measure.

| Strong. | Weak. | Strong. | Weak. | Strong. | Weak. | Strong. | Weak. |

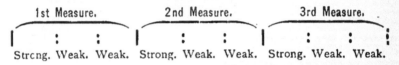

THREE-PULSE MEASURE.

1st Measure.	2nd Measure.	3rd Measure.

| Strong. | Weak. | Weak. | Strong. | Weak. | Weak. | Strong. | Weak. | Weak. |

UNIT OF TIME. The pulse is the natural *unit* of time, and by it the length of all tones is calculated. Thus tones are said to be one pulse, three pulses or half-a-pulse in length.

The advantages of the Tonic Sol-fa notation of PICTORIAL NOTATION OF TIME. time cannot be overrated. A reference to the above diagram will show that it gives prominence to the three principal facts referred to: each pulse being separately indicated, represented of equal length, and the various degrees of accent marked by specific signs. The following will serve still further to illustrate the unique character of this pictorial notation of time :—

Whole-pulse tones, .. |d   :d |d   :d |

Two-pulse tones, .. |d̄   :— |d   :— |

Half-pulse tones, ... |d .d :d .d |d .d :d .d ||

Quarter-pulse tones, .. |d,d.d,d:d,d.d,d| d :— ||

Pulse-and-half tones, |d :— .d |d :— .d ||

The notes which occupy a full space are one pulse in length; the dash (—) prolongs a tone into the following pulse; the dot placed in the centre of a pulse divides it into halves, and the comma divides the halves into quarters. The dash followed by a dot lengthens the tone by one half pulse. In the more intricate divisions of the pulse the pictorial character of the notation is preserved throughout.

TIME NAMES.

In order to convey a correct impression of the rhythmic divisions of the pulse, various "time names" are employed. These are exceedingly useful in introducing any new division of the pulse, as they establish, in the mind, an association of *syllable* and *rhythm*, in the same manner as Sol-fa names establish an association of *syllable* and *interval*. For full explanation of time names see page 48.

FINGER-SIGNS FOR TIME.

Some teachers use finger-signs for teaching time, but we do not recommend them except as an alternative means of illustration with very young pupils. For the convenience of those who may wish to use them, a diagram is provided on page 7.

CHAPTER IV.

THE VOICE.

"MAN has sought out many inventions," and has exercised wonderful ingenuity in the devising and constructing of many beautiful and apparently perfect musical instruments, but far above the works of man stands a beautiful and perfect instrument of wondrous mechanism, supplied to every individual by the Divine Maker, who planned it—the human voice. Among the many instruments made by man, there is not one which receives so little care and cultivation, or has experienced so much neglect as the human voice.

Many attempts have been made to compare the voice to a mechanical instrument, but when pushed to a legitimate conclusion every one has completely broken down. For the purposes of illustration, no one will serve our purpose better than the reed organ. In

| THREE ESSENTIALS OF THE VOICE. |

it we have the three essentials of vocal tone ; viz., bellows, vibrator, and resonator. In the organ, the wind is supplied to the vibrators by the bellows, and according to the pressure of wind from the bellows will the tone be soft or loud, and any irregularity of pressure will result in unsteadiness of tone. In the organ the vibrator is composed of steel reeds of various lengths, which, being set in motion by the wind from the bellows, emit a steady musical tone. The resonator is composed of sounding boards and hollow boxes, and likewise of the case of the instrument as a whole.

THE BELLOWS. In the human voice, the bellows are represented by the lungs. These are enclosed in the chest, which they fit exactly, and of which they occupy by far the largest portion, leaving but a small place for the heart. They are two in number, and are much wider at the bottom than at the top.

Underneath the lungs is the midriff or diaphragm, a muscular, movable partition by which the lungs are **THE DIAPHRAGM.** separated from the abdomen. It is arched upwards like an inverted basin, and when its muscular fibres contract, it flattens and descends, thus increasing the capacity of the chest at the expense of that of the abdomen.

Respiration consists of two acts, viz., inspiration and expiration. Inspiration may be produced in three different ways :—

(1) By pushing the chest forward and flattening the midriff, so as to compel the lungs to *descend*, and to increase in volume, in order to fill the empty space created by this movement.

(2) By extending the ribs *sideways*.

(3) By *drawing up* the upper parts of the chest, viz., the collar-bones and shoulder blades.

We will term these (1) Midriff breathing ; (2) Rib breathing ; (3) Collar-bone breathing.

COLLAR-BONE BREATHING INJURIOUS. Collar-bone breathing is to be condemned, and should never be used. It utilizes only the thin upper parts of the lungs,

which cannot contain as much air as the broad under
parts ; and, as all the parts surrounding the upper
region of the lungs are hard and unyielding, much
fatigue is occasioned by their use.   Midriff and rib-

| MIDRIFF AND RIB-
BREATHING DESIRABLE. |

breathing combined forms at once
the most natural and easy method of
breathing, and should be diligently practised by all.

The Vibrator is formed by two chords or bands
called the vocal ligaments.   These are enclosed in the
larynx, or voice box, commonly called Adam's Apple.*
To give anything like a full description of these ligaments would necessitate much more space than is
available, consequently we will merely analyze the
results of their action.   Sound " middle C " of the

| THE REGISTERS. |

piano and sing *downwards*, when a
change will be experienced in the
larynx and a difference in quality of tone will be at
once apparent, when A is sounded.   This is caused by
a change in the method in which the ligaments are
made to vibrate.   Continuing downwards no other
alterations will be experienced.   Starting from C and
singing upwards other changes will be felt between
E and F, and between B and C ; still another change
takes place between A^1 and B^1, but the register above
is not found in adult male voices.   The term *register*
has been given to each series of notes produced by
one mechanism, and the voice has been classified as
follows :—

---

* For full information, see " The Mechanism of the Human
Voice," by Behnke.   (Curwen & Sons, London, Eng.)

TABLE OF THE AVERAGE COMPASS OF THE REGISTERS.

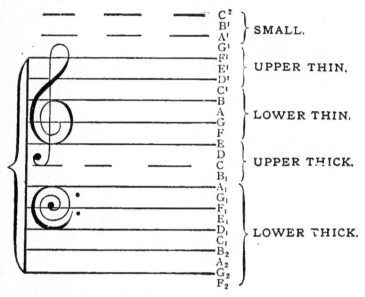

The names *thick*, *thin*, and *small* are given on account of the manner in which the vocal ligaments vibrate. In the thick registers, they vibrate throughout their whole *thickness*, but in the *thin* register, only the *thin* inner edges of the vocal ligaments are in vibration, and in the *small* register, only a *small* portion of the ligaments are in vibration.

The forcing of any of these registers *upwards* past the above limits is highly injurious, but they can be extended *downwards* without injury, and ought to be cultivated downwards until they blend with the register immediately underneath.

The *Resonator* is formed by the upper part of the throat and the mouth. To illustrate the functions of the resonator, take an ordinary violin string. stretch over an ordinary deal box, and set it in vibration.

A musical sound will certainly be produced, but poor in comparison with that which will be heard with the same string stretched over a violin. There is no difference in the vibrator—the string—but there is a great difference in the resonator. In the same way, let a person sing with the teeth nearly close together, the lips drawn over the teeth, the tongue arched upwards, and the breath kept back in the mouth, and we get a tone as poor in quality as any combination of salt box and fiddle string can make. But let the mouth be well opened and the voice directed well forward in the mouth, and we get a tone equally pure with that of the finest violin.

To produce a steady tone, and gain proper control of the breath, breathing exercises must be practised until a fair command of the lungs is obtained.

To produce correctly, tones of any pitch, we must study the action of the vibrator, until the registers of the voice are equalized and blended with each other.

Purity of tone depends largely on the shape of the resonator, the quality changing with the slightest motion of the mouth or throat.

In order to cultivate pure quality of tone, voice exercises should be practised at the *beginning of every music lesson.* By this means the attention is confined exclusively to the formation of correct habits in singing, which are thus kept before the mind throughout the entire lesson.

CHAPTER V.

MODULATOR DRILL.

IN the Tonic Sol-fa notation the modulator takes the place occupied by the staff in the common notation. Like the staff it gives a pictorial representation of intervals, but with more accurateness than is possible with the staff. The exact intervals between the tones of the scale are clearly shown in the first three steps, and in the following steps the true relation of keys, the most important element in the teaching of singing, is clearly set forth. Modulator drill should form the basis of all teaching to read music, and should occupy a prominent place in every lesson.

| HAVE AN AIM. | The teacher should have some definite object in view while con- |

ducting modulator drill. Some teachers simply let the pointer wander up and down as fancy may dictate. This is, unquestionably, wrong. The object of the drill should be :

1st. To familiarize the pupils with the mental effect of the tones, irrespective of the interval by which they are approached.

2nd. To enable the pupils to gain a clear mental conception of each tone, and to sing them in any desired combination.

3rd. To give confidence and certainty in points where a weakness has been found to exist. The methods of accomplishing this object are explained under modulator drill in the graded lessons given below.

Always sing the key-tone as a pattern to your class and do not commence drill until it has been imitated in correct tune by all.

If pupils experience a difficulty in singing any tone, do not tell them that they are singing too high or too low, but appeal to their sense of mental effect by questioning—Was that bright enough for *soh?* Did you sing that firmly enough for *doh?* Point definitely to the note you intend should be sung, and move the pointer rapidly to the note which follows.

Do not allow pupils to sing any tone until you have indicated it. A neglect of this rule will cause confusion and induce carelessness and inattention. Pupils *will* anticipate, but they must be trained to sing the intervals indicated by the teacher, not those which they expect. If a pupil should persist in this, either through carelessness, or eagerness, it will be advisable to request him to stop singing for a little. When one voice sings a wrong tone in advance of the others they are almost certain to follow, unless accustomed to singing with certainty.

AVOID REPETITION. In order to make modulator drill effective, repetition must be avoided. Inexperienced teachers frequently fall into the error of pointing to the tones in a loose, careless manner, whereby they unconsciously repeat phrases, and teach their pupils to anticipate the tones which follow. Such careless habit should be rigidly guarded against as it only leads to running in grooves, and instead of

RUNNING IN GROOVES. strengthening pupils in reading music, has a decidedly weakening effect. We have repeatedly seen classes singing apparently difficult exercises from the modulator, while their own teacher pointed, but when led by a stranger they failed completely to sing even the simplest intervals. On such occasions the teacher usually expresses surprise, and asserts that, " they always sing that easily for me," and certainly they do, but only when approached in the *one* manner to which they are accustomed. We have seen an instance of a class which would invariably sing the first half-dozen tones **d m s m r d,** *even though naming other tones pointed by the examiner.* This was certainly running in grooves with a vengeance. Still, the teacher of the class in question had been trying conscientiously to teach her pupils, and was perfectly satisfied with the results, as they seldom made mistakes while following her pointing. Of course she was unaware that she had been giving only a few tones, continuously repeated, and that her pupils had practically learnt nothing from all the modulator exercises they had sung. In order to avoid the error the teacher should memorise

HOW TO SECURE VARIETY. sections of tunes by various writers, containing a sufficient variety of style, and introduce them into the exercises given on the modulator. In the same manner difficult phrases in any song under study may be worked into the exercise with advantage.

It will also be found of mutual advantage to exchange with another teacher. By this means, both classes are tested by a strange teacher, and any weakness which may exist is quickly discovered.

It has been said that "the modulator is to the Tonic Sol-fa system as the sun is to the solar system," but this is only true when the modulator is properly used.

VOCALISING.

This is the term applied to singing on one vowel. The vowel most commonly used is the broad *ah*, as it secures the most open quality of tone, and aids correct opening of the mouth while singing. This is sometimes termed *laa-ing*. Whenever pupils can sing the syllables with any degree of certainty, they should be taught to vocalise from the modulator and hand-signs. This induces concentration, a definite conception of tones, and is an excellent means of mental training. It forms the connecting link between sol-fa-ing and singing to words. Pupils must not be expected to vocalise difficult intervals at first, but should be drilled in singing easy exercises from the modulator, at a slow rate of speed, in order that they may have time to *think* each tone. When this power of *thinking* the tones has been developed the syllables may be dispensed with, except in cases of exceptional difficulty.

CHAPTER VI.

SIGHT-SINGING.

THOROUGH systematic drill in sight-singing should form an important part of every lesson. During the earlier lessons it will be found advisable to write the notes on the blackboard without any regard to rhythm, in order that undivided attention may be given to the difficulties of tune.

"ONE THING AT A TIME."

As in modulator drill, repetition or running in grooves must be carefully avoided. In order to secure variety, extracts from songs which are unfamiliar may be taken and interspersed with phrases of the teacher's own composition

As a rule, the exercises should be short and to the point. Long exercises containing difficult intervals are dry and uninteresting, and are productive of little else than listlessness and restlessness. On the contrary, when short exercises, containing each a single difficulty, are used, the interest can be sustained for a much longer period. At the successful termination of each exercise there is a feeling that something has been accomplished, some difficulty overcome, and fresh difficulties are attacked with vigor and certainty.

SHORT EXERCISES ARE PREFERABLE.

Individualizing should be encouraged from the earliest lessons. At first nervousness and timidity will prevent pupils from volunteering to sing in presence of their classmates,

CULTIVATE INDIVIDUAL SINGING.

but a little discreet persuasion will soon convince them that individual singing is no more difficult than individual reading. Until a sufficient degree of confidence has been developed, it will be necessary to have the exercise sung by the entire class before being sung by individual pupils. When this stage has been reached, individual sight-singing may be attempted. While one pupil is reading the exercise, the others will be watching closely and eagerly listening for mistakes. This will be found an excellent means of cultivating habits of observance and attention in sight-singing.

Whenever an exercise has been satisfactorily sung on any one key, change the key, giving the sound of **CHANGE KEY FREQUENTLY.** the new *doh* firmly, and repeat the exercise. Pupils should be trained to sing in any key from the outset. Exercises which strain the compass of the young voices must not be attempted.

In primary classes it will be necessary to use the syllables almost exclusively at first, but the power to vocalise, *i. e.*, sing on one vowel-sound, should be developed simultaneously. Pupils may sol-fa an exercise easily, but unless they can afterwards vocalise, or sing it to words, the exercise will not be productive of the best practical results. Exercises containing exceptional difficulties should not be introduced unless there is a certainty that the pupils have sufficient ability to overcome them successfully. No fixed rule can be given for grading the difficulty of exercises in sight-singing for all classes, but the following will be found useful as a test. If pupils cannot vocalise an exercise after having sol-faed it three times, it may be safely assumed that it is too difficult. The intervals with which the difficulty has been experienced, should then be carefully studied from the modulator before being again introduced into the sight-singing exercises.

The use of colors in writing the exercises will be found helpful in many ways. They serve to recall the mental effects of the tones by comparison and contrast, and also concentrate the attention on the difficulties to be overcome.

CHAPTER VII.

TIME.

IN children the feeling of rhythm is instinctive and usually active. When a lively air is heard it will be

| INSTINCTIVE FEELING OF RHYTHM. |

noticed that children invariably incline to mark time in some way or other; it may be by stamping with the feet, nodding the head, clapping hands, or, if at liberty to do so, by marching in time with the music. Notwithstanding this fact, the number of classes in which " singing out of time " predominates, is largely in excess of those in which singing in strict time is the rule.

Several theories have been offered in explanation, all of which are more or less correct. One is, that pupils are not all of the same temperament, and those who are of a lively temperament will naturally incline to sing faster than those of a dull, sluggish disposition. This is certainly true, but when pupils are trained to take the rate of movement from the teacher's baton, all such individualities ought to be subordinate to the will of the teacher. This should be insisted upon from the most elementary lesson.

We are of opinion that the true cause of failure in teaching rhythm will be found in the unconscious habit, which many teachers have formed, of teaching *mathematics* of time, while the *thing* itself has been left untouched. In examination papers in music, we have frequently met with such

| MATHEMATICS MIS- |
| TAKEN FOR RHYTHM. |

questions as the following: "How many eighth-notes are contained in a dotted whole-note?" and have found pupils who could answer such questions correctly, but who could not tell the difference between the rhythm in "Old Hundredth" and "God Save the Queen," except on paper. Such examples of neglect of the precept which demands that "the thing before the sign" should be taught, are unfortunately by no means rare. In teaching time, it will be found advisable to develop the rhythm by listening to ear exercises, and tapping the pulses (see page 17), until a clear conception of the rhythm has been formed. When this has

| EYE-TRAINING. |

been satisfactorily accomplished, the pupils will be enabled to give undivided attention to the training of the eye in reading the notation of time.

In order to test the instinctive feeling of rhythm,
let the teacher mark the pulses, by tapping lightly,
while singing one or two measures containing intricate divisions of the pulse.   If this be sung on one
tone, it will be found that a majority of the pupils
will imitate correctly whatever phrase has been sung.
This experiment proves that there is little difficulty
in singing certain intricacies of rhythm, but *recognis-
ing* them in musical notation, and knowing *when* to
sing them is a very different matter.   In the ordinary
or staff notation of music this is a matter of consider-
able difficulty, and though it has been simplified to a
great extent in the Tonic Sol-fa notation, careful
attention to eye-training is absolutely indispensable.

The most common cause of difficulty is to be found

REGULARITY OF BEATING PULSES. in irregular beating of pulses in the
elementary lessons.   Teachers should
be careful to point to the *accent marks only* when conducting exercises in rhythm, and never on any
account to the notes, dots or commas contained within
the pulse.   The following will serve to illustrate the
proper and improper methods of pointing.   The *
denotes the position of the pointer at each successive
tap :—

Improper
Method.
|d   :r .r |m   :— .r |d   :t₁.t₁|d   :—   ‖

Proper
Method.
|d   :r .r |m   :— .r |d   :t₁.t₁|d   :—   ‖

Should the above improper method of pointing to
pulses be followed, it will be impossible to secure

correctness in singing in time. In writing on the
blackboard it will be found advantageous to use

**COLORED CRAYONS
ADVANTAGEOUS.** colored crayons for the pulse signatures. By this means they are made
to stand out distinctly from the notes, (which are
written with white), and the eye is unconsciously
directed to the sign for each pulse as it is felt or heard.

In teaching rhythm all exercises should be sung on
a monotone. This does not necessarily imply that
only one *note* should be used, Many teachers make
the mistake of using only one note, as follows :—

$$|d \quad :d \,.d\ |d \quad :— \quad |d\,.d\ :d\,.d\ |d \quad :— \quad \|$$

$$\text{or,}\ |1 \quad :1 \,.1\ |1 \quad :— \quad |1\,.1\ :1\,.1\ |1 \quad :— \quad \|$$

The first example is certainly preferable to the
second, but both fail in one important respect, viz.,

**USE MORE THAN ONE
NOTE IN WRITING.** eye-training. We have followed the
above method for years, but have
been compelled to abandon its use for the more
rational one of presenting the notation as nearly as
possible as it is likely to be met with in singing real
tunes. Examples of tunes consisting of a monotone
are exceedingly rare. If pupils are trained to sing
any new division of rhythm from a notation of one
note only, they experience a difficulty in recognizing
the same division in an unfamiliar melody. In order
to overcome this difficulty, we have adopted the
plan of changing the notes with every pulse, which
presents the notation in its true form and trains the

pupils to recognize it more readily when singing at sight. In pursuance of this plan the above exercise would be written—

|d :m .m|s :— |s .s :m .m|d :— ||

and would be taught first by using the time-names, then naming the syllables, *on one tone*, and finally singing the syllables in tune.

THE NOTATION OF TIME.

In a previous chapter reference was made to the educational advantage of the Tonic Sol-fa notation of time, in presenting a picture of the relative length of each tone, and clearly indicating each variation of accent.

Music, like poetry, is characterised by a regularity of rhythm and accent. To this fact we owe much of the pleasure which we derive from music; it may be

| REGULARITY OF RHYTHM. |

in the mere jingle of a minstrel ballad or the elevating strains of a grand oratorio. The influence of rhythm in music is all-powerful; but without it music would sound insipid and dull. Let the following familiar tune be sung with the strong accent on each note marked with a ^ and notice the effect.

KEY F   ST. PETER.

^   ^   ^ ^ ^   ^   ^
s d' t l s s f m m r d f m r

^   ^   ^   ^ ^   ^   ^
m f m l s s f m d m r d t, d

It will be apparent that the tune is altered almost beyond recognition by this simple change of accent.

By simply putting the accent on the second note and every alternate note following, the tune will be restored to its original form.

| ACCENTS. |

In the Tonic Sol-fa notation, provision is made for three gradations of accent, viz., *strong*, *medium*, and *weak*. The signs employed to represent these are

Strong | A relatively long upright line.

Medium | A relatively short upright line.

Weak : A colon.

MEASURE.

The strong accents recur at regular intervals and divide the music into *measures*. A measure is the space from one *strong* accent to the next *strong* accent.

In writing, the signs for the various pulses are placed at equal distances apart, and thus present to the eye a picture of the equal length of the pulses as recognized by the ear. Too much care cannot be observed in this particular, as an exercise in which

| PULSE SIGNS SHOULD BE EQUIVALENT. |

the pulses are represented as of unequal length is misleading, and is invariably sung in a halting and jerky manner.

The most common cause of this error is the habit of writing the notes and the pulse signs simultaneously.

| HOW TO WRITE. |

In order to avoid this, the signs for the strong pulses should first be written, then the measures divided into pulses, and finally the notes inserted in their respective places, moderately close to the pulse sign which *precedes* them.

EXAMPLE :—

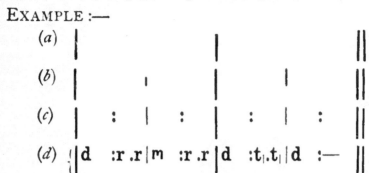

The above process may, on first sight, be considered rather slow, but on trial it will be found to take less time and secure better results than the haphazard method previously mentioned.

FORMS OF MEASURE. Measures are broadly divided into two forms, viz., *duple* and *triple*.

In *duple* measure every *alternate* pulse is accented.

In *triple* measure every *third* pulse is accented.

Two-pulse measure is the simplest duple form.

TWO-PULSE MEASURE.

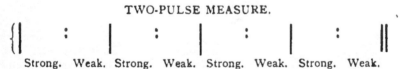

Strong. Weak. Strong. Weak. Strong. Weak. Strong. Weak.

Three-pulse measure is the simplest triple form.

THREE-PULSE MEASURE.

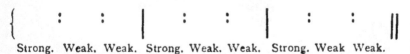

Strong. Weak. Weak. Strong. Weak. Weak. Strong. Weak Weak.

Occasionally the second pulse in three pulse-measure is sung with a medium accent, but it is always written as above.

FOUR-PULSE MEASURE.

Strong. Weak. Medium. Weak. Strong. Weak. Medium. Weak.

This is the most common of all forms of measure, and on this account is often termed " common time." The difference between the medium and strong accents is very slight, and by many performers both are made of equal importance.

SIX-PULSE MEASURE.

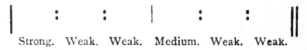

Strong. Weak. Weak. Medium. Weak. Weak.

This is sometimes termed double-triple measure, and it is important to note that it is composed of two sets of three pulses, not three sets of two pulses.

NINE-PULSE MEASURE.

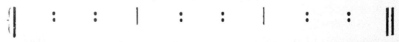

This is composed of three sets of three pulses each. It is not very commonly used, except in extended compositions.

TWELVE-PULSE MEASURE.

This is composed of four sets of threes, and like the previous form is not commonly used. Neither is likely to be found in compositions for school classes.

The double line at the end of the examples must not be mistaken for a pulse sign. It is used solely to denote the end of a complete piece of music, or section of such.

The bracket { denotes the end of a printed line or
score, and may include one or more parts. When
several parts are included within the { they are
intended to be sung simultaneously by voices divided
into a corresponding number of parts. In writing,
(unless where a silent pulse follows) a line should
never end with a pulse sign, as

{|d   :m.d |s   :m |r   :d.r |m   :d |

s   :f m |r   :m.f|m   :r |d   :—||

but should have the pulse sign placed at the beginning of the succeeding line. The reason for this is
that a pulse mark denotes the degree of accent to be
given to the note which it immediately *precedes*,
hence the pulse sign should not be in one line while
the note is in another.

SECONDARY MEASURES. When a piece of music commences
on the strong accent, as shown in
above examples, it is said to be in *Primary measure,*
and when it commences on any other than the *strong*
pulse it is said to be in *Secondary measure.*

EXAMPLES OF SECONDARY MEASURES.

Two-pulse   { : | : | : | ||

Three-pulse { : | :   : | : ||

Four-pulse   { : | : | : | : | ||

Six-pulse   { : | :   : | :   : | :   : | : ||

The criterion of a pulse is held to be that place in a piece of music where we instinctively beat time.

RAPID MOVEMENT OF PULSES. If a piece of music be performed alternately slowly and quickly, it will be found that in the latter case the stronger accents only will impress themselves sufficiently to be recognised as pulses, and the former pulses will be considered simply as sub-divisions of the new pulses. The most frequent use of this method is to be found in connection with six-pulse measure. When sung BEATING TWICE IN A MEASURE. rapidly this will appear to be two-pulse measure, with pulses divided into thirds. In beating time the beats will fall only on the strong and medium accents, thus :—

When it is intended that a piece of music should be sung in this way, directions as to beating time are given. " Beating twice in a measure," "beating twice,' or more frequently only the word "twice" is used to denote the method of marking the pulses.

In quick nine-pulse measure the pulses are beat " thrice in a measure," and are expressed as above, the word " thrice " being substituted for " twice."

METRONOME RATE. In order to denote the rate of speed at which pulses are intended to move in a given tune, Metronome marks are placed at the beginning, or at any point where a change in the rate of movement is desired. Metronome is the name applied to an instrument which marks the pulses at various desired rates of movement. Metronome 60, abbreviated M. 60, denotes that sixty beats of the Metronome are to be given in one minute.

Practically the M. may be taken to mean minute, thus M. 60, M. 70, M. 84, denotes that the number of pulses indicated are to occupy one minute.

M. 60 TWICE.

{| : : | : : ||

This indicates that the pulses are beat twice in each measure, moving at the rate of sixty pulses in the minute.

The more elaborate metronomes are supplied with a clock-work arrangement, and pendulum with sliding weight, which regulates the rate of movement according to a given scale. By means of a series of tooth-and-pinion wheels the pulses are ticked audibly, and some have a bell attachment which strikes the accented pulses also. Such instruments are rather expensive for general use, and a cheaper form of instrument is necessary. What is known as the "tape-and-weight" metronome will be found to answer all ordinary purposes. This is easily made by attaching a

| HOW TO MAKE A METRONOME. | weight to the end of an ordinary tape measure. This may be held in the |

hand, or suspended from any convenient peg, and when in motion each *complete* vibration will correspond to a pulse.

The following table gives the number of inches of the tape required for the different rates of movement.

The number of inches here given is not absolutely correct, but is near enough for ordinary purposes :—

M. 50........Tape 56 inches.
M. 56........ "   47   "
M. 60........ "   38   "
M. 66........ "   31   "
M. 72........ "   27   "
M. 76........ "   24   "
M. 80........ "   21   "
M. 88........ "   17   "
M. 96........ "   13½   "
M. 120........ "   8½   "

In order to gain some idea of the respective rates of movement, it is advisable to memorize one distinct rate, and adopt it as a standard by which to compare all others. M. 60 will be found most serviceable for this purpose. When this rate has once been fixed in the mind, it will be an easy matter to think of M. 120 as being twice as rapid, M. 90 one half quicker, and the intermediate rates in proportion.

BEATING TIME.

Various methods of beating time are employed as :

1. Tapping the blackboard while pointing to the pulse-signs of the tune being sung.

2. Tapping the pulses audibly without pointing to the pulse-signs.

3. Stamping with the feet.

4. Simply marking the pulses by a clearly defined movement of the pointer or baton.

The first two methods are necessary in conducting elementary exercises, in which the pupils' attention is concentrated on the notation, but should be dispensed with as soon as possible.

The third method is unquestionably bad, and has not one single redeeming feature to recommend it. When indulged in, it induces loud and harsh singing with consequent forcing of voices. Teachers should discourage its use on the part of their pupils, and should avoid setting a bad example.

NOTE.—This is easier said than done.

The fourth method is the best of all. Pupils should be thoroughly trained to watch the beat, and no exercise or song should be considered well taught until it has been sung in accordance with the silent movements of the teacher's baton ; in this respect the teacher must be an autocrat, by whose will every pupil must submit to be governed.

The ordinary forms of beating time are as follows:

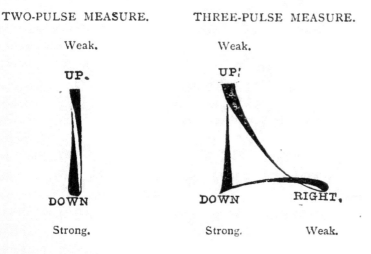

TWO-PULSE MEASURE.	THREE-PULSE MEASURE.
Weak.	Weak.
UP.	UP!
DOWN	DOWN RIGHT.
Strong.	Strong. Weak.

FOUR-PULSE MEASURE.

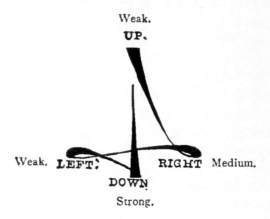

SIX-PULSE MEASURE.

Down, left, left, right, right, up.

Sometimes this is beat as for two three-pulse measures. When quick, beat as for two-pulse measure.

NINE-PULSE MEASURE.

Commonly treated as three-pulse measure. ·

In beating time, the baton should move quickly, and definitely to a "point of rest" at the extremity

> MARK TIME
> DEFINITELY.

of each beat. The tendency to indulge in cutting ornamental figures should be carefully avoided. This style of conducting is unfortunately too common. It may seem to be pretty enough when viewed by an audience of spectators, but the teacher must remember that he conducts, not for the *audience*, but for the *singers*. No style of marking time can rivet the attention of the singers so well as the plain geometrical movement of the baton indicated above. In order to define the rate of movement, it is advisable to beat a silent measure before the singers commence. As a rule this should begin on the first pulse of the measure, and should the piece begin on a secondary measure the voices will enter when due.

LENGTH OF TONES.

All duration values are calculated from the pulse as a unit. A note placed between any two pulse-signs is one pulse in length, unless followed by some qualifying sign.

EXAMPLE :—

|d :s |m :d |r :t, |d :d |

Each note in the above is one pulse in length. When a tone is continued or prolonged, a continuation mark (—) is written in the pulse or pulses through which it is intended to be continued.

EXAMPLE :—

|d :— |s :— |m :— |— :— |

In the above, **d** and **s** are each two pulses, and **m** is four pulses in length. In writing the notation, the continuation mark should be placed equidistant from the dots of the colon, or opposite the centre of the upright bars, but must not touch either. See above example.

CONTINUATION MARKS.

The Tonic Sol-fa notation gives a common-sense representation of silence or rests. Where there is nothing to be sung, nothing is represented, consequently no signs what-

RESTS.

ever are used to denote silences. The number of
pulses or fraction of pulses which is left *empty* denotes
the duration of the silence or rest.

EXAMPLE :—

$$|\text{d} \quad :m \quad |s \quad : \quad | \quad :m \quad |d \quad :— \quad ||$$

In the above the third and fourth pulses being
empty, denotes a two-pulse silence.

| DIVISION OF |
| PULSES. |

Pulses are divided into fractions by
signs placed between the pulse signs.
A dot placed in the middle of a pulse, on a level with
the lower dot of the colon, divides the pulse into
halves.

EXAMPLE :—

$$|\text{d} \quad :d\,.r \quad |m \quad :r\,.d \quad |r \quad :d\,.t_| \quad |d \quad :— \quad ||$$
$$\tfrac12\ \tfrac12 \qquad \tfrac12\ \tfrac12 \qquad \tfrac12\ \tfrac12$$

The ½ shows the notes which are half a pulse in
length. Notes are frequently continued for one half
pulse only ; such continuation is represented by a
short continuation mark.

EXAMPLE :—

$$|\text{d} \quad :-\,.r \quad |m \quad :-\,.r \quad |d \quad :-\,.t_| \quad |d \quad :— \quad ||$$
$$1\tfrac12 \qquad 1\tfrac12 \qquad 1\tfrac12$$

Pulses are divided into quarters by placing a
comma in the middle of each half-pulse.

EXAMPLE :—

$$|\text{d} \qquad :r\,,m\,.f\,,s \,|1 \qquad :s \qquad ||$$
$$\tfrac14\ \tfrac14\ \tfrac14\ \tfrac14$$
$$|\text{d}^| \qquad :s\,,f\,.m\,,r\,|d \qquad :— \qquad ||$$
$$\tfrac14\ \tfrac14\ \tfrac14\ \tfrac14$$

Combinations of halves and quarters are represented as follows :—

HALF AND TWO QUARTERS.

| d :r .m,f | s :s .f ,m |
½ ¼ ¼

| r :r .m,r | d :— ||

TWO QUARTERS AND HALF.

| d :r ,m.f | s :s ,f .m |
¼ ¼ ½ ¼ ¼ ½

| r :r ,m.r | d :— ||
¼ ¼ ½

In representing the division of the pulse into three-quarters and quarter, a slight deviation has been made from the consistency of the notation, as explained above. Formerly the three-quarter-pulse tone was treated as a half-pulse tone continued for an additional quarter pulse, and represented as such by a short continuation mark extending to the comma, thus :—

| d .– ,r :m ||

The majority of teachers however, have now decided that the three-quarter-pulse tone should be considered as a thing in itself, and not a half-pulse tone continued. In addition, the above form of notation was found to be inconvenient to the printer. The continuation mark has now been discarded, and the dot placed almost close to the comma.

EXAMPLE :—

| d :r .,r | m :r .,m
¾ ¼ ¾ ¼

| f :m .,r | d :— ||
¾ ¼

The division of the pulse into thirds is represented by *inverted commas*.

EXAMPLE :-

$$|d \quad :r \,{}_,r \,{}_,r \,|m \quad :r \,{}_,r \,{}_,r \,|d \quad :t_{|} \,.t_{|} \,|d \quad :— \quad \|$$
$$\qquad \tfrac{1}{3}\tfrac{1}{3}\tfrac{1}{3} \qquad\qquad \tfrac{1}{3}\tfrac{1}{3}\tfrac{1}{3}$$

Any part of a pulse may be *silent*. The space left empty will denote the part of the pulse which is *silent*.

EXAMPLE :—

$$|d \quad : \quad .r \,|m \quad : \quad .r,m|f \,.\,{}_,s\,:m\,,\,.\,{}_,r\,|d \quad :— \quad |$$
$$\qquad \tfrac{1}{2} \qquad\quad \tfrac{1}{2} \qquad \tfrac{1}{4} \qquad \tfrac{1}{4}\tfrac{1}{4}$$

A complete time-chart for reference is given on page 8.

TIME-NAMES.

The above written analysis of time-values cannot convey any correct impression of their effect when sung. This can only be learnt through hearing. Every teacher who has experienced the difficulties of teaching *Rhythm*, must realise the advantages of a system of "Time-names," which at once gives a clear conception of the mental effect of various rhythmic forms, and fixes their conception on the ears and minds of the pupils. The time-names of the Tonic Sol-fa system have been adopted from M. Paris's "Langue des durees," which had previously been successfully used in France in connection with the "Galin-Paris-Cheve" system. This system is in many respects identical with the Tonic Sol-fa system and is based

on the same fundamental principles. The Time-names
have been adopted by the promoters of other systems,
but have been so improved (?) as to be almost un-
recognisable. The beautiful simplicity of the arrangement of the vowels has been discarded, and a separate
vowel introduced on every accent. The mere effort
of memorizing such a complex arrangement of *names*
induces confusion and neglect of the *thing*. When
the founder of the Tonic Sol-fa system,—Rev. John
Curwen,—first adopted the French time-names he
was induced to improve (?) on them by changing the
consonants, and in several instances the vowels also ;
but his experience, and that of the large body of
teachers of the system, resulted in a return being
made to the simple names, as proved and tested by
the French for years. In announcing his decision he
says, " If names become complex they draw a large
amount of attention to themselves, which should be
given to the things they represent. In carrying the
time-names through a course of lessons, I found that
my modifications, simple as they seemed, had introduced a practical complexity which became more
troublesome than useful, and that increasingly so as
we went further on. Therefore it was after long
discussions and experiments that we decided to use
the French time-names just as they came to us after
years of well-tested use." The Time-names have now
been in use for sixty years, and, in their original form,
are more generally used than ever.

" The system is founded on the principle that time
is measured to the ear and mind, not by appreciated

durations only, but by those louder and abrupt deliveries of tone which we call *accents*—both by the stronger accents of a measure and by the more delicate accents of a pulse." The time-name for the *first stroke* of a pulse is *Taa*, and, should no qualifying sign be added within the pulse, no additional syllable is necessary. Consonants indicate the *percussion* of tones, vowels indicate their *duration.* The following are the time-names for the common divisions of rhythm :—

WHOLE-PULSE TONES.

|d   :r |m   :d ||
Taa   Taa   Taa   Taa

HALVES.

|d .r   :m .d |r .m   :d .d ||
Taa - Tai   Taa - Tai   Taa . Tai Taa - Tai

QUARTERS.

|d ,r .m ,f :s ,f .m ,r |d   .t| :d ||
Ta fa te fe Ta fa te fe Taa   Tai Taa

HALVES AND QUARTERS.

|d .r ,m :f   .m ,r |m ,f .s   :d ||
Taa te fe Taa te fe ta fa Tai Taa

THREE-QUARTER AND QUARTER.

|d   .,r :m   .,f |s   .,f :m ||
Taa . fe Taa - fe Taa - fe Taa

THIRDS.

|d ₍r ₍m :r ₍m ₍f |m ₍f ₍s :d ||
Taa tai tee Taa tai tee Taa tai tee . Taa

The Time-names for silences are formed by substituting *s* for the initial consonant, thus—

d	:	|m	.	:d	.	||
Taa	Saa	Taa	Sai	Taa	Sai	

|Saa	.d Tai	:r Taa	. se	,m fe	|f ,m Ta fa	. se	,r fe	:d Taa	. Sai	||

The time-names for continued tones are formed by simply omitting the initial consonant, thus :—

|d	:—	|r	:—	.d	||
Taa	-aa	Taa	-aa	Tai	

|d	:— ,r .m ,f	|s	:—	.f ,m	||
Taa	-a fe te fe	Taa	-aa	te fe	

|d	:— ,r ,m	|f	:— ⸌ ,m	||
Taa	-aa tai tee	Taa	-aa -ai tee	

NOTE.—" Ai " is pronounced as in m*ai*d, f*ai*l, etc.: " aa " as in father ; " a " as in m*a*d ; " e " as in l*e*d, and " ee " as in tr*ee*.

For time-names of more intricate divisions of the pulse, see Time-Chart on page 8.

In practice, the time-names are sung on a monotone. It must be borne in mind that they are simply a means to an end, and not, as has sometimes been claimed, the " *Ne plus ultra* " in teaching time. We have frequently met with classes which could sing the most complicated rhythms while using the time-names or *laa* on one tone, but stumbled wofully when attempting to sing in tune simple exercises, containing no greater difficulties of rhythm than half-pulses. Such results are invariably caused by a false interpretation of the principle of teaching " one thing at a time." The elements of *Time* and *Tune* should invariably be taught separately until each has been mastered, but should then be immediately combined. When a certain division of rhythm has been mastered, and can be readily sung at sight on one tone, it should be combined with various tune-forms and practised thoroughly. Until this has been accomplished, it is unwise to introduce any new or more difficult form of rhythm.

CHAPTER VIII.

EAR CULTIVATION.

IN the foregoing chapters we have confined the attention almost entirely to the *reading* of music; but now an equally important subject remains to be discussed, viz., the *thinking* of music.

The importance of this factor of musical education cannot be over-estimated. We have frequently met with instances of persons who could read music, but who could not tell the names of tones by ear, but have never known anyone who could name tones by ear without being able to sing them readily at sight. Many teachers have the impression that the faculty of recognizing tones by ear is difficult of acquirement, and can only be acquired by the gifted few. The unvarying experience of practical teachers is that any pupil who can recognize the difference between a high tone and a low one, can be trained to distinguish minute intervals of tune and time, provided the course of training be systematic and thorough.

The Tonic Sol-fa system of ear-training is based on the doctrine of "mental effects" of tones in key, not on the effects of tones in absolute pitch. One of the ablest of American musical critics, in an article on the subject, says :—"The current impression of the average American writer on this subject, that the main feature of the Tonic Sol-fa system is the simple | A CRITIC'S OPINION | notation, leaves entirely out of the | OF SOL-FA METHODS. | question two other elements, which are, if possible, even more important. The first of these elements is the method of instruction, or of cultivating the ear, invented, systemized and perfected by the Tonic Sol-fa teachers. They have the only system of training the ear to a cognition of musical impressions, according to their real nature, possessed by any body of elementary teachers."

Exercises in "ear-telling" should form a part of every music-lesson. These exercises cultivate quickness in the sense of hearing, and in perception of tone relation ; and, in addition, cultivate the powers of observation and analysis. Pupils who have been trained on this principle can usually see more in a | CULTIVATE INTELLI- | musical composition than those whose | GENT OBSERVATION. | powers of reading only, have been cultivated. The latter are usually found lacking in the analytic faculty in observing. Just as in viewing a landscape, a cultivated eye will see beauties which to the ordinary observer are invisible, so also in reading music. Pupils should be trained, not to be mere singing machines, but to be observant listeners and intelligent performers.

| EAR EXERCISES ASSIST THE VOICE. | These exercises are also valuable from the fact that they give certainty |

to the voice in reading music. Many teachers make the fatal mistake of teaching singing by the same methods as they teach playing on an instrument. In playing, the reading of the notes is simply a matter of *location*, *i. e.*, reading the positions of the notes upon the staff and *locating* them upon the keyboard of the instrument. This may be accomplished mechanically by persons utterly devoid of musical feelings ; but the reading of music in singing is a very different matter. No person can produce a vocal tone without first having formed a definite *conception* of the tone to be produced. In training the mind to form this conception, ear exercises are of the utmost importance.

They are also helpful in testing individual pupils in musical examinations. Written examinations in music are frequently valueless as an indication of musical ability, while individual examinations of a practical nature are as frequently misleading. In the

| USEFUL AS AN EXAMINATION TEST. | state of nervousness consequent on the consciousness of being under |

examination, pupils cannot be expected to do justice to themselves or their teacher, as they frequently lose control of the voice altogether. The ear exercises supply a practical test which is a happy medium between written and oral examinations, combining the advantages of both, while being freed from their disadvantages.

While the advantage of these exercises cannot be

gainsaid, it is a matter of regret that, of all subjects in the musical curriculum, this receives the least attention. The reason is not far to seek. The majority of teachers consider the subject too difficult, and are afraid of making mistakes while conducting the exercises. Teachers of ordinary musical ability can easily overcome this difficulty by attending to the preparation of the lesson. This may be done by memorizing a few phrases, suited to the grade to be taught, and using them as ear-tests. Three or four such tests will be sufficient for a first attempt. When these have been used successfully, confidence will result, and exercises containing greater difficulties may gradually be introduced.

ALL TEACHERS CAN LEARN TO TEACH MUSIC. Unfortunately, however, there are many otherwise excellent teachers who have been denied the advantages of an early musical education, and consequently cannot, with any degree of confidence, use their voices in teaching to sing. Many will unhesitatingly condemn such teachers for attempting to teach music, saying they ought not to be allowed to do so ; but to this I most emphatically take exception. In this enlightened age they are few persons who will deny the utility of music-teaching in the school-room, or its advantages as a means of educational recreation. Granted that it possesses the advantages which have been claimed in its behalf, are teachers to be deprived of the enjoyment of sweet sounds, solely on account of an inability which is no fault of theirs? Most certainly not. I have had the privilege of being associated in the

work of teaching with many such teachers, and have
yet to learn of one who could teach other subjects
satisfactorily and has failed with music, after a
conscientious endeavor to attain the necessary pre-
liminary qualifications.   Such teachers may never
acquire sufficient confidence to enable them to sing
in presence of their pupils, but they undoubtedly can
cultivate the power of detecting errors in singing, by
studying under a competent teacher.   For the benefit
of such teachers the following methods have been
devised.

Cultivate the habit of vocalising in your pupils.

This will enable them to *think* the tones indepen-
dent of their names.   Encourage pupils to do this
individually.

If pupils display special aptitude in this direction
let them sing an ear-test while the others write the
names of the tones.   Example.—A girl satisfies the
teacher that she is competent to vocalise a phrase of

| PUPILS ASSIST THE TEACHER. |

four tones.   She writes them on her
slate, and takes a position in front of
class.   Pupils are directed to write on their slates the
numerals 1, 2, 3, 4, and to listen for the fourth tone.
The girl will then vocalise the four tones, say **d s m d¹**.
Pupils will then write the name of the fourth tone
under number 4.   This will be repeated while they
listen for the third, second, and first tones, respectively,
when the correct names will be announced.   If this
exercise be carefully conducted, pupils will be eager
to assist and will probably display more interest than
when the exercise is sung by a teacher.

A musical instrument may also be used with advantage. If a piano or organ is available, so much the better; but if not, there are other less costly

INSTRUMENTAL AID IN EAR-TRAINING. instruments which will serve the purpose equally well. There is a suitable little instrument called the " Metalophone," which can be procured at a moderate cost. It is composed of a sounding box made of wood, on which strips of metal of various lengths are loosely nailed. These, when struck with a small hammer, produce distinct musical sounds which can be distinguished readily by ear. In purchasing, it will be necessary to select one which is strictly in tune, as the inferior sorts are apt to be wofully deficient in this respect.

Detailed hints for conducting ear-exercises will be found in subsequent chapters.

CHAPTER IX.

SCHOOL SONGS.

IN the preceding chapters we have simply described the methods of conducting exercises in the various elements of music, but their successful combination into a complete whole demands a special treatment of its own. In teaching music there is a constant

DANGERS OF STUDYING EXERCISES ONLY. danger of sacrificing everything to *technique*, to make singing automatons of our pupils, rather than to lead them to see and

feel the beauties of song, and so give intelligent expression to the sentiments of the poet and composer.
In order to gain this desired end, exercises, in Tune,
Time, Ear-training and Vocal Gymnastics, must certainly be studied, but simply as a means to an end.
As a means of developing the powers of observation
and concentration, of cultivating readiness in reading,
and agility in executing, so that the mind may be
relieved of all thought of merely mechanical details,
and be at liberty to think of the more æsthetic
qualities of music. If our choice were limited to
exercises without songs, or songs without exercises
we should certainly choose the latter ; but fortunately
the Tonic Sol-fa system provides an excellent means
of securing both. A properly selected song, well
taught, provides an excellent means of training at
once the voice, the ear and the mind.

In order that a song may possess those educational
advantages it must be adapted to the abilities of the
pupils, must contain no difficulties of Tune or Time

SELECTION OF SONGS. which have not been previously mastered by a series of carefully graded
gymnastics. It must also contain no tones outside
the limits of the range of the pupils' voices, and above
all the sentiment of the verse must be such as the
pupils can easily comprehend. No true teacher would
for a moment, think of giving an exercise in reading
from the Fourth Book to the pupils of the Primary
class, still the equally un-educational method of
teaching (?) fourth-step songs to junior pupils is being
pursued every day.

If songs are adapted to the abilities of the pupils, their study is certain to be a delightful source of pleasure and interest ; they will be found humming them around the school·yard, or singing them in the home for the entertainment of their parents, where, probably, their influence will create more true happiness than the most brilliant warbling of the *prima donna*. The use of songs in the school-room fulfils the double purpose of providing instruction and recreation in the most pleasing form. Most teachers can testify to the benefits derived from singing some well-known school song when pupils have become tired and restless from close application to more severe studies. Such benefits will be impossible of attainment, however, should the singing of the song entail the study of any serious technical difficulties. Let the songs selected be such as have been described above, and let them be preceded by a carefully graded series of exercises, and the singing lessons will be remembered as being among the brightest in school-life. An excellent authority on teaching has observed that " Our pupils remember us, not from the amount of technical knowledge with which we may have been able to cram their minds, but from the pleasure which we have combined with the acquirement of that knowledge." If we desire to make school-life thoroughly enjoyable, alike for pupils and teachers, let us have it freely interspersed with suitable songs which will teach only the true, the noble and the good.

It·must not, however, be supposed that only pupils

who have learned to read music are to be allowed to sing. Such a course would be altogether contrary to nature. Children learn to sing at their mother's knee by the simplest of all methods, viz, *imitation*, and this should be continued throughout the earlier period of school-life. Our aim, as teachers, should be to continue the imitative process begun in infancy, so that the children may never know the time when they *could not sing*. This can best be accomplished through the free use of Rote Songs, consisting of simple words of easy comprehension, enlivened by a

| ROTE SONGS. |

bright "taking" melody. In teaching a song by rote, the teacher must be careful to avoid loud or harsh singing, using only a pure, sweet tone of voice. The time should first be taught without the words, the teacher *alone* singing the first phrase *while the pupils listen*. When one phrase has been correctly imitated, the next will be taught by the same method until the whole tune has been learnt. The words should be studied separately from the teacher's pattern. In teaching the words, it is advisable to recite them on a *monotone*, but with exactly the same *rhythm* and *accent* as will be used when singing in tune. When this has been accomplished the words and music should be combined, and the ideas contained in the words developed by appropriate questioning. A number of suitable Rote songs will be found in the Appendix.

| ACTION SONGS. |

Rote songs are frequently sung in combination with appropriate actions, and are then known as Action Songs. By many

teachers, Action Songs have been unhesitatingly condemned, and by others they have been equally unhesitatingly endorsed. It cannot be denied that when
singing is accompanied by appropriate actions, or
gestures, the general effect is enhanced and rendered
exceedingly pleasing. The actions, likewise, usually
consist of calisthenics, designed with the view of pro-
moting æsthetic physical culture, and development of
what has been fitly termed the "poetry of motion." As
such, they are certainly productive of beneficial results,
and are worthy of encouragement within reasonable
limits. The great danger attending their use lies in
the tendency to subordinate the *musical* to the *general*
effect. This leads to the formation of careless habits
in singing, and consequent misuse of the voice. In
trained operatic artists, we have the highest type of
singers of Action Songs. Even they, though trained
to the scientific use of the voice, tell us that the strain
on the physical and nervous system is much greater
on the operatic stage than on the concert platform,
where gestures are not generally used. If this be the
case with adults, specially trained for this particular
work, and possessing the knowledge requisite to
govern the various faculties which it calls into action,

DANGER OF
ACTION SONGS.

how great must be the danger atten-
dant on the singing of Action Songs
by little children, whose physical organs are as yet
weak and undeveloped. In Action Songs the gestures
should be quiet and natural, and the singing soft and
sweet. The teacher who cannot secure attention to
these essentials, should not attempt the teaching of

Action Songs. Their use can be entrusted with safety only to the teacher who can realise the extreme delicacy of the vocal organs, and the care necessary to their successful preservation and development.

If the object be the study of calisthenics, that only should engage the attention of the pupils. I have seen a class of children with backs bent and hands outstretched in the endeavour to touch their toes, and while in this position actually attempting to sing. Of course freedom of breathing under the circumstances was an impossibility. I do not for a moment object to calisthenics in the school-room, being aware of the beneficial results following their intelligent use; but when calisthenics are being practised as such, I am of the opinion that the music necessary to the definition of a rhythmical accompaniment should not be supplied by the performers themselves. In order to supply the necessary accompaniment, a musical

CALISTHENICS AND SINGING.

instrument may be used. If a piano or organ should not be available, the mouth organ, metalophone, or even the tap of a toy drum, will be found serviceable. Failing these, one half of the class may sing the accompaniment while the other *silently* practise the exercises. By this means they can study the actions of the others and learn sufficient for their performance when the others have finished.

CHAPTER X.

SYLLABUS OF MUSIC FOR GRADED SCHOOLS.

REFERENCE has already been made to the division of the system into "Steps," and the necessity of adhering to the plan of teaching contained therein. In order to adapt the system to the ordinary divisions of Public and High Schools, a more minute sub-division is necessary. Some writers favour the plan of teaching music in three divisions only, viz., Primary, Intermediate, and Advanced, and combining several classes of various grades under each division. Under exceptional circumstances this may be a convenient arrangement, but it has numerous disadvantages. Pupils who have already mastered the elements of the "step" are compelled to practice with others who have not, which is liable to induce lack of interest in the one class, and mere dependence and rote-singing in the other. There is also the additional disadvantage of loss of time in combining several classes in one room, and the increased difficulty of securing and maintaining discipline in large classes. Better results can be secured when the exercises are adapted to the ability of each class, and superintended by the regular teacher. This will necessitate the division of the subject into at least eight separate grades, in accordance with the classification usually adopted in grading the ordinary subjects of the school curriculum. While the classification is practically the same in all Canadian Public Schools, there exists a lack of uniformity in the terminology employed to designate the various classes. In order to prevent the confusion inseparable from an adoption of the terminology of any particular locality, we will simply provide a syllabus for 1st Division, 2nd Division, etc. This can be adapted to any system of grading which may be desired. The subject has been divided into six branches, each of which should receive special attention.

Many teachers devote the time of the music lesson almost exclusively to sight-singing and the practice of songs, to the exclusion of ear exercises and time drill. In order to avoid this error, a monthly review should be held and marks given in each subject according to the degree of proficiency attained. This plan has been found to produce excellent results wherever tried. The pupils like to know exactly how they stand in all subjects, and when poor marks are given in any, an improvement is always noticeable at next review.

The following will be found useful as a guide in preparing for reviews. The subject of voice-training is placed last, and pupils must be cautioned against using harsh or impure tone, as the marks for this are given according to the quality of the tone shown in the previous subjects.

	MAXIMUM.
Modulator exercises - - - .. -	8
Time " - - - -	8
Sight-singing " - - - - -	8
Ear " - - - -	8
Prepared song - - - - - -	8
Voice-training - - - - -	10
Total - - - -	50

DIVISION I.

MODULATOR.—To sing from teacher's pointing, in any key, exercises on the **DOH** and **SOH** chords, including the upper and lower octaves of the tones d, m, s, t, r.

TIME.—To sing from pointing on blackboard, on one tone, exercises containing full-pulse, half-pulse, and continued tones.

To write on slates, from teacher's dictation, examples of two, three, and four-pulse measure.

SIGHT-SINGING.—To sing from blackboard, phrases of four, six, or eight tones composed of the tones, d, m, s, t, r, in any easy position.

EAR EXERCISES.—To tell, by ear, the name of any one of above tones, sung to **LAA** or numbers.

To *imitate* in correct tune and time, simple phrases of from three to six tones, containing divided pulses.

PREPARED SONG.—To be sung to words, with neatness of articulation, and soft, pure tone, an action-song learnt by rote.

To sing to words, a simple song composed of the tones d, m, s, t, r, learnt by note.

VOICE-TRAINING.—To sing *all* exercises and songs with softness and purity of tone, the mouth being opened neatly and naturally, and the tone produced well forward in the mouth.

NOTE.—The work prescribed for this grade has been made exceedingly simple, in order that *every child* may be enabled to accomplish it. Teachers will guard against attempting anything more difficult, as it is important that, at this early stage, the musical faculty, however dull, should be awakened and developed. Pupils who sing out of tune must *listen* attentively for some time, and will soon be enabled to sing with the others.

DIVISION II.

MODULATOR.—To sing from teacher's pointing *easy* exercises containing *all* the tones of the major diatonic scale.

TIME.—To sing on *one tone* to time-names, *laa*, or sol-fa syllables, exercises containing full-pulse, half-pulse, pulse-and-half, and continued tones, and full-pulse silences, written in two, three, or four-pulse measure.

SIGHT-SINGING.—To sing from blackboard easy phrases, containing *any* tones of the major scale.

EAR EXERCISES.—To tell by ear the name of any one tone of a phrase sung to *laa*, or numbers, the teacher previously sol-faing the tones of the **DOH** chord.

PREPARED SONG.—To contain the tones of second step of the Tonic Sol-fa system, viz.: **d, m, s, t, r**, learnt *by note*, and may include divided pulses.

Attention to be given to accent, enunciation, phrasing, quality of tone, and expression.

VOICE-TRAINING.—Same as for Division 1.

DIVISION III.

MODULATOR.—To sing from teacher's pointing, *in any key,* exercises of moderate difficulty containing leaps to all tones of the major scale, with special reference to **fah** and **lah**.

TIME.—To sing on one tone to time-names, or *laa*, sol-fa syllables, exercises containing divisions of time prescribed for Division II. with the addition of quarter-pulse tones and silent half-pulses.

SIGHT-SINGING.—(*a*) To sing from *blackboard*, exercises of moderate difficulty containing any tones of the major scale. (*b*) To sing from *books* any exercises containing the tones of the second step, but no divided pulses.

EAR EXERCISES.—(*a*) To tell by ear the name of any one tone of a phrase sung to *laa* or numbers, the key being frequently changed. (*b*) To sing from teacher's dictation, simple phrases of three or four tones, *i e.*, the teacher *says* d m r, pupils *think* the phrase, then sing in tune to syllables **d m r**. (*c*) To tell by ear, and sing to time-names, a short phrase containing any divisions of time mentioned above.

PREPARED SONG.—To sing from books any simple school song learnt by note. Attention to be given to accent, enunciation, phrasing, quality of tone, and expression.

VOICE-TRAINING.—Same as for Division I. and II., with addition of short tuning exercises in two parts.

———

DIVISION IV.

MODULATOR.—To sing from teacher's pointing in any suitable key, exercises containing difficult leaps to any tones of the major scale.

To sing from teacher's pointing with *two* pointers, simple exercises in two parts.

TIME.—To sing on one tone to *time-names*, *laa* or sol-fa syllables, and afterwards to sing, in *correct tune*, simple exercises containing any divisions of time specified for Divisions I, II, III.

SIGHT-SINGING.—To sing from blackboard, in correct *time* and *tune*, easy exercises containing any tones of the scale, with continued tones, but no divided pulses.

EAR EXERCISES.—(*a*) To tell by ear the sol-fa names of any *three* tones in stepwise order, sung to *laa*, or any other syllable. (*b*) To sing from teacher's dictation phrases of three or four syllables containing intervals of moderate difficulty. (*c*) To tell by ear, and sing to time-names, a short phrase containing any divisions of time mentioned above.

PREPARED SONG.—To sing from books, in *two parts*, any easy school song containing the tones of the third step, and easy divisions of the pulse. Attention to be given to accent, enunciation, phrasing, quality of tone and expression.

VOICE-TRAINING.—To practice exercises in correct breathing and tone production, with fair command of voice and attention to *piano* and *forte*.

NOTE.—Where the word *sing* is used above, singing to sol-fa syllables only is implied.

The syllabus for Divisions V. to VIII. will be found in Part II.

CHAPTER XI.

NOTES ON DIVISION I.

FIRST LESSON IN TUNE.

FIRST STEP
MODULATOR.

$\cdot$

m$^!$

$\cdot$

DOH$^!$

$\cdot$

SOH

$\cdot$

ME

$\cdot$

DOH

$\cdot$

$\circ$

s$_!$

$\cdot$

m$_!$

THE following is a condensed sketch of a first lesson in tune as actually given to a class of pupils in the Primary Grade:

INTRODUCTION OF SUBJECT. (*a*)

Teacher.—We are now about to have our first lesson in music, but before we begin, I want you to tell me just what you think music is. Is it something you can see? or taste? or hear?

Class.—Something we can hear.

Teacher.—Yes; music is something we can hear. What do we call anything which we can hear?

Class.—Sound.

Teacher.—Now I will drop this pointer on the desk, and you will tell me what you hear. (Drops it.) Was that a sound?

Class.—Yes.

Teacher.—Was it music?

Class.—No.

Teacher.—Then, clearly, all sounds are not music. Now listen while I sing a little piece, and tell me what kind of sound you hear. (Sings short, familiar air.) What kind of sound was that?

Class.—Nice sound, sweet sound, etc.

Teacher.—What kind of sound did yon hear when I dropped the pointer?

Class.—Rough sound, noisy sound.

Teacher.—Yes; all sweet, pleasant sounds are called music, and rough, harsh sounds are called noise. (*b*)

INTRODUCTION OF DOH.

Teacher.—Now that we have found out that music is sweet sounds, we will try and make some of those sweet sounds. You will listen while I sing one sound, and then you will sing it *after me*. (Sings *ah*, softly at moderately low pitch. Pupils imitate, and repeat.)

Teacher.—You will now listen while I sing two tones, and tell me whether they are the same in sound. (Sings *same ah* twice.) Did you notice any difference between those two tones?

Class.—No, they are the same.

Teacher.—Now try once more.

INTRODUCTION OF SOH. (*c*)

(Sings to syllable *ah*, two tones doh and soh, *i.e.*, the first *ah* given, and another a fifth higher.) Did you notice any difference between those two?

Class.—Yes; one was higher than the other.

Teacher.—Quite right. I will now give you the names of those tones. The low one we call **doh**, the high one **soh**. Now sing after me (sings **d s** and pupils imitate several times). I will now write them on the blackboard $\left\{ \text{Writes } \begin{array}{l} \textbf{soh} \\ \textbf{doh} \end{array} \right\}$ and you will sing them as I point. (Points to notes in any order while pupils sing as directed.)

INTRODUCTION OF ME.

Now you will listen while I sing to *ah* and tell me which of those tones I sing *last*. (Sings **d s d** to *ah*, then **s d s**, pupils naming last tone sung.) You seem to know those two very well. Try once more. (Sings **d s m** to *ah*.) (*d*) Now tell me which tone I sang last.

Class.—**Doh, soh,** new tone, various answers.

Teacher.—You do not seem to be quite sure this time; try again. (Repeats until pupils have all discovered that the last is a new tone.)

Teacher.—Can you tell me whether the new tone is above or below **doh**? above or below **soh**?

Class.—Between the two.

Teacher.—Quite correct. I will now write it for you and you will sing from my pointing. $\left\{ \text{Writes } \begin{array}{l} \textbf{s} \\ \textbf{m} \\ \textbf{d} \end{array} \right\}$ Gives tone **doh**; class imitate and attempt to sing each tone as pointed.

Mental Effect of Tones.

Teacher.—You seem to find it rather hard to sing them in any order, but I think when we learn something more about them you will find it much easier to sing them. Can you tell me if there are any little boys in this room so much alike that you can't tell one from another ?

Class.—No, they are all different.

Teacher.—Just so. When you look at a boy, you see at a glance what sort of a look he has on his face ; some boys have a nice, bright look, others a quiet, calm look, and others a firm, determined kind of look. It is just the same with those tones we have been singing, each has a character different from the others. You will now sing as I point, and think more particularly of **doh** while you sing, and try to tell me what kind of tone it is. (Points while class sing, giving prominence to **doh**.) Now can you tell me what kind of tone **doh** is? (Class will not answer correctly at once, but as a rule their answers will give some idea of the real character of the tone.)

Teacher.—I will now ask you to compare this tone with something you have already seen. Most of you have seen a mountain, a strong, firm, solid mountain. You have also seen a fountain, with its bright, sparkling, dashing waters. Now sing those tones once more and tell me which of the two **doh** is like. (Class sing from pointing as before.)

Teacher.—Raise hands, all who think **doh** is like a fountain. (No hands are raised.) Now all who think **doh** is like a mountain. (Nearly all hands are raised.)

Teacher.—I think you are all right ; will you tell me why **doh** is like a mountain ?

Class.—Because it is strong and firm.

Teacher.—Yes ! **doh** is the firm tone. I will write its character beside it so that you will think of it when you sing. { Writes **m** ^{s} d *firm.* }

(*e*) The teacher will now proceed to develop the mental effect of **me** and **soh** by the same process, comparing **me** to mother singing baby to sleep, and little brother singing loudly and waking baby. **Me** is calm and gentle. **Soh** is bright and bold and may be compared with a bugle in contrast with a drum.

PRACTICE.

The character of each tone being written on the blackboard

{ s *bright* }
{ m *gentle* } practice in singing slowly from teacher's pointing
{ d *firm* }

must now be given slowly, in order that pupils may feel the mental effect of the tones as they sing.

(*a*)   This is intended to awaken interest.

(*b*)   By this definition of music, pupils commit themselves, and later on when they sing loudly or coarsely, as children will, if not checked, their teacher will appeal to their former definition of music, and enquire whether they are now making *sweet sounds*.

(*c*)   **Soh,** being next in importance to **doh,** is next in order of introduction.

(*d*)   Sing the new tone very softly in order that the dullest pupil may recognize its introduction.

(*e*)   The earnest teacher will have no difficulty in inventing suggestive illustrations of the points to be developed, but in no case may the pupils be *told* the character of the tones.

NOTE.—In the above lesson the correct answers by pupils are given, but teachers must not expect such answers at first. The teacher must take what answers the pupils may give and lead them, as only a teacher can, into the desired channel.

FIRST LESSON IN TIME.

The following is a condensed sketch of a first lesson in time, as given to a class of pupils in the second school-year. It will be useful, where the teaching of music is being introduced for the first time, to classes of this or senior grades ; but where music is taught as a regular subject, during the first session of primary classes, the alternative lesson given below will be found more suited to the pupils' requirements.

Before proceeding to give the following lesson, the teacher must be prepared to sing some well-known tune with divided pulses and well marked accent.

Teacher.—In our previous lesson we learned to sing in tune the

INTRODUCTION.

tones **doh, me, soh,** but in music there is something to be studied besides *tune.* Listen while I sing and notice whether there is anything wrong with this tune, as it is sung. (Sings National Anthem with time and accent altered). Did that tune sound all right ?

Class.—No. It was all out of time.

Teacher.—Quite right. I will sing it once more while you listen. (Sings in strict time.) Did it sound any better last time ?

Class.—Yes. You sang in time.

Teacher.—I may now tell you that the " something besides **Tune**" which I referred to is *Time.*

I will now sing a tune which you all know, and while I do so you will clap hands gently. (Sings, " Home, Sweet Home," while pupils beat time as directed.) Can you tell me what it was that made you keep time together so nicely ?

Class.—It was the singing.

PULSES.

Teacher.—Yes. There is something in every tune which will enable us to keep time. This we call the *pulse* of the tune. I will sing another tune and you will beat time as before, that is, you will find out the pulses of the tune. (Sings several tunes of varying character in order to develop the fact that pulses exist in *all* tunes.)

REGULARITY OF
PULSES.

Teacher.—When I sang the first tune, did you notice whether you clapped hands for *every* tone that was sung ?

Class.—Yes, we did. (This answer, though incorrect, is almost invariably given.)

Teacher.—I will sing it once more, beating time for every tone. (Sings as indicated, pupils notice the incongruous and unnatural method of beating.) Is that how you beat time ?

Class.—No. We beat time more smoothly.

Teacher.—Your beating seemed more natural. Can you tell me whether the beats were regular or irregular ?

Class.—They were regular.

Teacher.—You will now find] out the pulses in several tunes, and notice whether they occur as regularly as before. (Sings examples of quick and slow tunes while pupils beat time.) Were the pulses regular in all of these tunes ?

Class.—Yes, but some tunes were slower than others.

Teacher.—This is a very important fact. I will illustrate it for you. You must all have noticed how a clock ticks and also how a watch ticks. Do both tick regularly?

Class.—Yes; but the watch ticks the faster.

Teacher.—It is exactly so with the pulses in music. In some tunes they move slowly, in others quickly, but in all they move *regularly*.

ACCENT OF PULSES.

There is still something to learn about pulses. We have found that they are all equal in *length*. Now we will see whether they are equal in *strength*. (Sings an example of tune in duple time.) Did you notice any difference in the strength of the pulses?

Class.—Every alternate pulse was strong.

Teacher.—Yes. The order of the pulses was strong, weak, strong, weak. You will now sing to the syllable *laa* after I have given you a pattern. (Sings LAA, *laa*, LAA, *laa*, repeatedly, after which pupils imitate.) All exercises in time only must be sung on *one tone*

NOTATION.

in order that it may be free from difficulties of tune. When pupils can sing readily with alternate strong and weak accents proceed to the notation of time.

Teacher.—I will now give you the signs for the pulses.

The pulse which has the strong accent is represented by an upright bar (|) and the weak accent by the colon (:)

Writes | : | : | : | : ||)

The double bar simply indicates the close of the exercise.

You will now sing as I point to the accent marks. (Class sing as directed, care being observed in sustaining the weak pulses for full length of time.)

MEASURE.

Teacher.—You notice how nicely the strong pulses seem to measure off the music into equal divisions. The space from one strong accent to the next strong accent we call a measure. Count the pulses and tell me how many we have in each measure.

Class.—We have two pulses in each measure.

Teacher.—This we call two-pulse measure.

In order to develop the accent, the above will now be contrasted with three-pulse measure in which the accents occur as strong weak, weak.

Written | : : | : : ‖}

PRACTICE. Now write four two-pulse measures, with one note in each pulse.

|d :r |m :r |d :t, |d :d ‖

Each note is sung loudly or softly according to the accent-mark which immediately *precedes* it.

TIME-NAMES. *Teacher.*—We have a series of time-names which you will find helpful in keeping correct time. When we have one note in each pulse we call it **taa.** (Writes **taa** under each note, gives pattern, and pupils imitate.)

Teacher.—Listen while I sing and tell me whether you notice any change. (Sings in one tone, prolonging the first tone in second and last measures.)

TWO-PULSE TONES. *Class.*—You made some tones too long.
Teacher.—In which measure did I do so ?
Class.—In the second and fourth measures.

Teacher.—I will give you the time-names for the prolonged tones and you will imitate. (Sings **taa taa taa-aa taa taa taa-aa,** and class imitate.)

Teacher.—The sign for a continued tone is the dash (—). (Rubs out fourth and last notes and substitutes the dash.)

Pupils will now be drilled in singing from teacher's pointing, using time-names and *laa.*

ALTERNATIVE FIRST LESSON IN TIME.

(FOR INFANT CLASSES ONLY.)

Teacher.—I am now going to sing a song which you all know, and while I sing you will clap hands softly.

(Sings bright kindergarten song in *duple* measure while pupils beat time.)

Teacher.—You will now sing the song yourselves and clap hands as you did before.

(Pupils sing as desired, while the teacher draws an upright line as the accented notes are sung.)

Teacher.—While you were singing I drew some lines on the board, and now I will tell you what we will do with them, we will make houses with them. Just count them, please, and tell me how many houses we have.

(Class count as teacher points, one, two, three, four.)

Teacher.—Yes; we have four houses with a big double wall at the end. Can you tell me how many rooms we have in each house?

Class.—One room in each house.

Teacher.—I am sure none of you little folks would care to live in a house with only one room. Can any one tell me how we can make these into two-roomed houses?

Class.—Build a wall in the middle.

Teacher.—Yes; that would do nicely. (Writes a short thick line in each house.)

Now we have two rooms in each house. I think that in every house we should have a play-room for little boys and girls, don't you think so too?

Class.—(Smiling,) yes!

Teacher.—We all know that when little folks are playing, they do not like to be kept too quiet, but enjoy making a noise and having a nice time, so we will have one of these rooms for a play-room, a noisy room. Suppose we decide on the one after the big, high wall for our noisy room. (Points to the first pulse in each measure, while pupils say noisy room.)

Teacher.—I want some one to point out all the noisy rooms. Who will do it?

(All are eager to point, teacher selects several who do it correctly in turn.)

Teacher.—Now listen while I sing, making *all* the rooms .oue noisy rooms. Does that sound nicely?

Class.—No.

Teacher.—Listen again and tell me whether you think this sounds better. (Sings with alternate strong and weak accents).

Class.—That sounds better; we like it better.

Teacher.—What difference did I make?

Class.—You made noisy rooms and quiet ones.

Teacher.—We will take the rooms behind the *little* wall for our quiet ones. Please name them as I count.

(Pupils name as requested.)

Teacher.—Who will point out all the quiet rooms?

(Pupils point out all the quiet or noisy rooms as desired.)

Teacher.—There is just one thing about our houses that I don't like. When we point from a noisy to a quiet room, we have to skip over the little wall. How can we improve that?

Class.—Make a door through it.

Teacher.—Yes, that will do nicely.

Erase part of each short line, leaving the required sign for the weak accent, thus :—

$$|\quad : \quad | \quad : \quad | \quad : \quad | \quad : \quad \|$$

Teacher.—Now, sing while I point to each of the rooms. (Sings pattern on one tone which pupils imitate).

We will now place one little boy in each of the rooms.

Writes, $|$ d :m $|$ s :s $|$ s :m $|$ d :d $\|$

When we have a boy in the noisy room, what sort of boy will he be?

Class.—A noisy boy.

Teacher.—Show me all the noisy boys. All the quiet boys? (Pupils point as desired.)

Teacher.—When we have just one boy in a room we call him TAA.

(Sings TAA *taa* TAA *taa*).

| TIME-NAMES. |

(Pupils imitate.)

Teacher.—Now sing the syllables on one tone.

(Class sing as desired.) Listen while I sing it and tell me whether I make any change. (Sings on one tone, continuing the first **s** in second measure, and first **d** in fourth measure.)

Class.—You missed some of the boys. You made some longer than others.

Teacher.—Quite right. This **soh** (indicates it) went right into the next room and **doh** did the same. We will put away the two which I did not sing. (Erases second **s** and last **d**). When we want a little boy to get through from a noisy room to a quiet room we will lay down a little carpet for him to walk on. (Writes continuation mark in empty pulses.)

Listen while I sing this and tell me what I sing in the rooms with the carpet. (Sings to time-names.)

Class.—You sang *aa*.

Teacher.—Quite right. You will now sing it as I did. (Class sing as desired.)

The exercise will now be sol-faed on one tone, then in tune from teacher's pattern.

By the above method, the pupils are led from point to point, as in an interesting story, and unconsciously learn the first elements of time, without being burdened with their nomenclature. The lesson is given in detail, all the above answers having actually been given by pupils of the infant class. The play-names used may be retained for some time, until the pupils can read from notes, then, as a reward for diligence, they may be told the real names, pulse, measure, etc.

The first introduction of a subject only occurs at intervals, and daily drill must succeed every such introduction. As the time available for teaching music is necessarily short, it will be our endeavor to assist the teacher to make the best possible use of it, by giving examples of methods of drilling in all the various topics.

MODULATOR DRILL.

Use a first step modulator, which is composed of the tones **d m s** only. If a printed step modulator has not already been procured, an excellent substitute can be made by writing the names of the tones in *colors* on the blackboard. If blackboard space is scarce, a movable modulator can be made of black Bristol-board, with letters cut from colored surface paper, and pasted on. The colors recommended are, **doh**—red ; **me**—blue ; and **soh**—bright yellow.

In first step exercises **doh** is always sung without difficulty, **soh** and **me** require special drill. The following illustrates the method :—

DRILL ON SOH.

Teacher sounds **doh** about pitch of D. (Pupils imitate softly.) Question on the mental effect of **soh**. Give hand-sign for **soh**. Teacher sings **d m d; s m d; m m d; d m m; m d m**. After singing each group of three tones, give hand-sign for **soh**, indicating that pupils will sing **soh**. In this exercise they confine their attention to the tone being studied, and become familiar with its mental effect. Now point phrases in which **soh** predominates.

EXAMPLE :—

d s m s s d s d s m s d s m d s.

DRILL ON ME.

Question on mental effect of **me** as above. Sing **d s m; m d s; s m d; d m s; d d s; s s d;** Pupils sing **me** from hand-sign after each group of three.

Now point phrases in which **me** predominates.

EXAMPLE :—

d m m d s m s d m m s m m d s m d.

Change key frequently, and vary the order in which the tones are approached. When mistakes are made, do not tell pupils to sing higher or lower, but question on mental effect, as, " Was that *bright* enough for **soh** ?" " Did you sing that gently enough for **me** ?" If this fails, the tone may be sung by the teacher, but not unless absolutely necessary.

NOTE.—See " Modulator, Drill " page 25.

SIGHT-SINGING.

EXAMPLES OF METHOD.

Teacher writes on board **d m d s m d s d**. Sings **doh**, key D. Pupils imitate.

Teacher.—Now sing from my pointing.

Class sing **d m** correctly, but sing second **d** like **soh**.

Teacher erases first and second **doh's** and rewrites with *bright red* crayon. Can you tell me what color this first **doh** is written with ?

Class (eagerly)—Red.

Teacher.—And is the second **doh** of the same color ?

Class.—Yes.

Teacher.—If the *color* of both **doh's** is the *same*, do you not think that the *sound* of both should be the *same* ?

Class.—Yes ; they should have the same sound.

Teacher.—Now try again, and be careful to give the second **doh** the same sound as the first.

Class sing correctly until second **s** is reached.

Teacher writes both **soh's** with bright yellow crayon and reasons as before. Also draws attention to bright character of **soh**.

When the exercise has been correctly sung by the entire class, the boys and girls may be asked to sing separately, next by one row at a time, and finally by individual pupils.

When the exercise has been correctly sol-faed, it should be sung to *laa*.

KEY EXERCISES.—KEYS C TO G.

d	s	s	m	s	d	m	m	d
m	d	s	m	d	d	s	s	d
s	s	m	s	d	d	m	s	m
d	m	d	s	m	s	s	d	d
d	d	m	d	s	m	d	s	m

In teaching sight-singing, *Tune* and Time may occasionally be combined in such a manner that only one topic will demand attention.

EXAMPLE :—

| Teacher writes | d | :m | s | :— | s | :m | d | :— | ‖ |

Class sing to time-names, then to syllables in tune, making **s** only one pulse in length. This is a common mistake with young pupils. Teacher shows that **s** should be continued through the fourth pulse, and sung *soh oh*. It may be useful to write *oh* under the continuation-mark. When this has been sung correctly the *tune* should be changed, the time-form is retained.

EXAMPLE :—

a.	d	:m	s	:—	s	:m	d	:—	‖
b.	d	:s	m	:—	m	:s	d	:—	‖
c.	m	:d	s	:—	s	:d	m	:—	‖
d.	s	:m	s	:—	m	:d	m	:—	‖

NOTE.—See " Sight-Singing," page 79.

TIME.

The object of time-exercises at this stage should be—

1st. To develop an appreciation of the regularity of pulses and accents in music.

2nd. To enable pupils to distinguish between tones of one, two or more pulses in length.

3rd. To train the eye to read the notation of above divisions of rhythm.

EXAMPLES OF METHOD.

Pupils clap hands softly while singing *taa, taa, taa* on one tone, taken at any rate indicated by teacher's pointer. When a change is made to a faster or slower rate of speed, the singing must cease while the teacher counts a few pulses at the rate required.

Vary the exercise by changing the measure frequently. Pupils count ONE, *two*, ONE, *two* ; or ONE, *two, three,* ONE, *two, three,* with emphasis on ONE.

When this has been sufficiently well sung, pupils may be requested to sing two-pulse measure or three-pulse measure, the teacher simply indicating the rate of movement without giving any special sign for the strong accent.

Short exercises containing few difficulties will be found the most useful in training the eye and ear in teaching time.

Write the following exercise on the blackboard :

Ex. 1.　KEY D.

$$|\text{d} \quad :\text{m} \quad |\text{s} \quad :\text{s} \quad |\text{s} \quad :\text{m} \quad |\text{d} \quad :— \quad ||$$

Question on Measure, Accent, Length of Tones and Time-names.

Direct pupils to sing to Time-names on one tone, to sol-fa on one tone and to sol-fa in tune. When this has been sung successfully, intimate that a change will be made, and request pupils to watch closely while this is being done. Alter the exercise into

Ex. 2.　KEY D.

$$|\text{d} \quad :\text{m} \quad |\text{s} \quad :— \quad |\text{s} \quad :\text{m} \quad |\text{d} \quad :— \quad ||$$

Question on alteration. Direct pupils to sing to Time-names and sol-fa, as above. Whenever the exercise has been correctly sung, it should be altered and taught as above. The Time-names may be gradually discontinued, as the pupils gain confidence in sol-faing at sight. The order in which the tones are first given, should be preserved throughout (repeated tones excepted), in order that no difficulties of tune may interfere with the study of time.

The "unexpected" will be the chief source of difficulty in this form of exercise. It has been said that "the ear *remembers* and *expects*." This truism will serve to explain one-half of the difficulties to be met with in teaching music. Let the above exercise be altered into

$$|d \quad :m \quad |s \quad :- \quad |m \quad :- \quad |d \quad :- \quad \|$$

and note the result. It will, almost invariably, be noticed that the m in third measure will receive one pulse only, and displacement of accent will consequently ensue. The explanation of this is to be found in a comparison of the first two with the last two measures. Every tune, however simple, divides naturally into at least two

| THE UNEXPECTED. |

sections, which should be combined according to a definite rhythmic or melodic form. In the *first* section of the above exercise, we have an example of the rhythm *taa, taa, taa, aa,* which is followed by a change of rhythm in the *second* section. In singing this, the ear *remembers* the rhythm of the first section and *expects* the same in the second section, hence the surprise and consequent confusion when *taa, aa* is met with instead of *taa, taa.* Exercises of this sort should be freely used in order that pupils may form the habit of singing what is written for them regardless of the unexpected.

Example of exercises to be studied on above plan:

Ex. 1. KEY D. Primary two-pulse measure.

a.	d	:m	s	:s	s	:m	d	:—	‖
b.	d	:m	s	:—	m	:—	d	:—	‖
c.	d	:—	m	:—	s	:m	d	:—	‖
d.	d	:m	s	:s	m	:—	d	:—	‖
e.	d	:m	s	:—	—	:m	d	:—	‖
f.	d	:—	—	:m	s	:m	d	:—	‖
g.	d	:—	m	:s	s	:m	d	:—	‖

Ex. 2. KEY D. Secondary two-pulse measure.

a.	:d	m	:—	s	:m	d	:—	—	‖
b.	:d	m	:m	s	:—	s	:m	d	‖
c.	:d	m	:—	—	:s	m	:—	d	‖
d.	:d	m	:s	s	:—	—	:m	d	‖
e.	:d	m	:—	—	:m	s	:m	d	‖
f.	:d	m	:m	s	:—	—	:m	d	‖
g.	:d	m	:—	s	:—	m	:—	d	‖

Ex. 3.   KEY C.   Primary three-pulse measure.

a. | d :d :d | m :m :m | s :s :s | d¹ :—:—||

b. | d :— :d | m :— :m | s :— :s | d¹ :—:—||

c. | d :d :d | m :—:— | s :s :s | d¹ :—:—||

d. | d :d :d | m :— :m | s :— :s | d¹ :—:—||

e. | d :— :—| m :m :m | s :— :—| d¹ :—:—||

f. | d :— :d | m :m :—| s :s :—| d¹ :—:—||

g. | d :d :—| m :— :m | s :s :—| d¹ :—:—||

The last example may be written in secondary three-pulse measure by beginning on the last pulse of the measure and deducting
one pulse from the last note, thus :

a. :d | d :d :d | m :m :m | s :s :s | d¹ :—||

Where pupils experience a difficulty in singing continued tones,
they may be allowed to intensify the vowel sound in each continuation.   In this manner a **doh** which is three pulses in length will be
sung as **doh-oh-oh**, and **me** as **me-ee-ee**.

SPECIMEN LESSONS.

Before introducing the subjects contained in the
following lessons, pupils should have had sufficient
drill in the primary lessons in tune and time to enable
them to read at sight exercises consisting of the three
tones **d m s** arranged in any order, and also any combinations of one and two-pulse tones in two-pulse
measure.

Assuming that satisfactory progress has been made we will now introduce the

SECOND LESSON ON TIME.

Write on blackboard four two-pulse measures,

| : | : | : | : ||

Teacher.—Please sing as I point. Be careful to sing the accents distinctly. (Pupils sing to *laa* as requested.)

Teacher.—What name do we give to the space between one strong pulse and the next strong pulse ?

Class.—A measure.

Teacher.—How many measures have we on the board ?

Class.—Four.

Teacher.—How many pulses are contained in each measure?

Class.—Two.

Teacher.—Will some one please point out the first measure, the third, etc. ? (Volunteers point out each measure as required.)

Teacher.—Name the pulses in this measure.

Class.—Strong, weak, strong, weak, etc.

Teacher.—Now listen and tell me if I sing the pulses exactly as we have them here. (Sings to *laa* with accent on first pulse of every group of three, LAA, *laa, laa*, LAA, *laa, laa*.) How did the pulses sound as I sang ?

Class.—Strong, weak, weak.

Teacher.—You will now sing them in exactly the same manner. (Pupils sing from pattern, teacher tapping time lightly.)

Teacher.—I will now write from your dictation the signs for the pulses as we have just sung them. What is the sign for the strong pulse ?

Class.—A bar.

Teacher.—For the weak pulse ?

Class.—A colon.

Teacher.—And what have we next ?

Class.—A weak pulse : a colon.

Writes as directed,

| : : | : : | : : | :: ||

Teacher.—Now count and tell me how many pulses we have in each measure.

Class.—Three.

Teacher.—This we will call three-pulse measure. Listen while I sing, and tell me whether I sing two or three-pulse measure. (Alternates two and three-pulse measure until pupils are familiar with the accents in each and can detect them readily.)

Four-pulse measure will be taught by same method, the accents being strong, weak, medium, weak. The sign for the medium accent is a short bar, thus :

$$ | \quad : \quad | \quad : \quad \| $$

DIVIDED PULSES.

Write as formerly four two-pulse measures.

Teacher.—Sing this exercise to *time-names*. Sing it to *laa*. (Pupils sing as requested). Now listen and tell me whether I sing it correctly. (Sings it to *laa*, putting *two* tones in second pulse.) Did I make any mistake ?

Class.—Yes.

Teacher.—Will some one point out the pulse in which mistake was made ? How many tones did I sing in second pulse ?

Class.—Two.

Teacher.—Listen once more and tell me whether those two tones are equal in length.

Class.—They are equal.

Teacher.—I will now let you hear the time-name for a pulse divided into two equal parts, and you will sing it after me. (Sings **TAA Taa-tai, TAA Taa-tai,** and pupils imitate). Now that you can sing it I will show you the sign for a pulse divided into halves. (Writes two notes in second pulse with a period between and time-name underneath, thus :

$$ \begin{array}{c} \text{:d .d} \\ \text{Taa-tai} \end{array} \Big| .) $$

Practise singing to time-names and *laa* on one tone, and alter frequently, placing half-pulse and continued tones in any order.

EAR EXERCISES IN TIME.

EXERCISES IN TIME. I will now sing a phrase and you will listen and tell me how often you hear **taa-tai**. This is done at first on one tone to *laa* and then a short *tune* containing divided pulses may be sung, if the pupils show sufficient aptitude in detecting **taa-tai** when sung on one tone.

LESSON ON OCTAVES.

Teacher.—In our previous lessons we have studied three tones, but there are still several others to study. Listen while I sing, and tell me whether you hear anything that sounds *like* a new tone. Sings to

OCTAVE OF DOH.

laa **d m s d**, in the key of D or C.

Class.—There was no new tone.

Teacher.—Listen once more (sings **d m s d¹**, the last **d** being an octave higher than the first.)

Class.—The last one was a new tone.

INTRODUCED BY EAR EXERCISES. *Teacher.*—Quite right. Now sing these four tones *after* me. (Gives pattern and class imitate.) Was the new tone higher or lower than **soh**?

Class.—It was higher.

Teacher.—Sing the phrase again and tell me whether it sounds like any of the other tones?

Class.—It sounds like **doh**.

Teacher.—It really is **doh**, but being sung so much higher it sounds like a new tone. I will now explain how we happen to have one **doh** so much higher than the other. In the scale of music we have but *seven* primary tones, just the same number, you will see, as we have days in a week. We begin the week with Sunday, and end it with Saturday. When we reach the last day of the week, what day do we have next?

Class.—We have Sunday again.

Teacher.—We do exactly the same thing with the tones of the scale. (Draws diagram on blackboard). Here we have the tones already learned with dots in the place of those not yet introduced. Can you tell me where to put the new **doh**?

. 7
. 6
s 5
. 4
m 3
. 2
d 1

Class.—It should be above number seven.

Teacher.—Yes! it is the eighth tone. (Adds **d 8**). The interval from any tone to its eighth is called an octave, and in order to distinguish the upper **doh** we write the figure *one* above it, then we see that it has to be sung *one octave* above **doh**. (Writes **d¹**.)

DRILL.

Pupils will now be drilled in singing from teacher's pointing on the modulator, exercises containing the upper **doh** in combination with the other tones. There will be no difficulty in teaching the mental effect of the new tone, it being firm and strong as **doh**, but rather brighter owing to difference in pitch.

CHANGE THE KEY.

The octaves of **soh** and **me** will next be introduced, care being taken to change the key in order to have the tones within the range of the pupils' voices.

INTRODUCTION OF SECOND STEP.

a s d ; d m s d ; d s t.

Teacher.—How many tones have we now learnt in music?

Class.—Three ; **doh, me** and **soh.**

Teacher.—And how many tones have we in the scale?

Class.—Seven.

Teacher.—Now that you have studied the three named, and can sing them readily, we will study some of the others, and then we will be able to have even prettier tunes than we have been singing recently.

EAR EXERCISES.

Listen while I sing four tones, and tell me whether you hear any new ones. While I sing, I will point to each of my four fingers, and if you should hear a new tone you will be able to tell me on which number it is sung. (Sings to *laa*, after giving key-tone, **s m s d**; **s m s m** ; questioning whether new tone has been heard after singing each phrase. The next phrase will have the first three tones same as before, but the fourth will be **ray**, which is a fourth below **soh**.) Did you hear any new tone?

Class.—Yes ; the fourth one.

Teacher.—Quite right. I will repeat the phrase, and you will

INTRODUCTION OF RAY.

sing it after me. (Class imitate as desired.) Can you tell me where to put the new tone, whether above **doh** or **me**?

Class.—Between **doh** and **me**.

Teacher.—That is its right place. The name of the new tone is **ray,** and I will now write it on our modulator. It is spelt **r-a-y,** but as we only use the initial in our notation, we will write **r** only. (Writes **r** between **d** and **m** on modulator.) You will now practise this new tone from my pointing. (Points to the tones in the following order, **s m s d s r r s r m r d r.)** You seem to have some difficulty with the new tone, but I think you will find it as easy as the others when you have studied its character. Listen while I sing, and tell me what kind of a tone you think **ray** is. (Sings **s m s r r s r m d r,** emphasizing **r.)** Can anyone describe its character?

m¹
d¹
s

m
r
d

s¹

MENTAL EFFECT OF RAY.

Class.—Loud; noisy.

Teacher.—Yes, I did sing it rather louder than any of the others, but any tone can be sung loudly equally well. Let me try and help you with a little illustration, One day last summer, while passing a nice lawn, I saw two boys. One was running around playing with his ball, but the other was lying asleep. The boy who was playing did not seem to care about playing alone, so he went up to the other and tried to rouse him up, but the other boy was too lazy, and just rubbed his eyes a little and said, " Just leave me alone, will you, I want to sleep." Here we have two boys, one dull and lazy, the other lively and rousing. Which of the two do you think **ray** is most like?

Class.—The rousing boy.

Teacher.—Yes, **ray** is a rousing tone, and if you think of it as such you will find little difficulty in singing it when required. (Writes the word rousing opposite **r,** and drills on the modulator, giving prominence to the new tone.) The next tone to be introduced is **te,** which is immediately below **doh.** Adopt same method as in introducing **ray,** being careful to approach it from **soh.** The mental effect of **te** is sharp and piercing, and may be illustrated by a steam whistle, a pen, or a scream.

The tones **s t r** will now be practised in the same manner as **d m s,** to which they are closely allied, the intervals being exactly similar. (See Chordal Treatment, page 16.)

MODULATOR DRILL.

The intervals **d¹ m** and **s₁ m** are the most difficult in the first step, consequently should receive special attention.   In a modulator voluntary intended to teach these intervals the mental effect of **m** should be clearly established, and the tone itself repeatedly sung, in order that it may be clearly fixed on the ear and mind before being approached from **d¹** or **s₁** The effect may be intensified by a pause being made on **m** wherever it occurs in the exercise.

EXAMPLES OF EXERCISES:—

KEY D.

d m d s m m s m s d¹ m m d¹ m s d

KEY G.

d m d s₁ d m m s₁ m s m s d s₁ m m d

It will be advisable to frequently contrast the effect of **m** with **s**, as **s** is the tone most frequently sung in place of **m**.   Care must be observed to keep the exercises within the compass of the young voices.   The extreme upper note which may be taken is E¹, but until pupils have acquired the habit of using the upper thin register (see page 23) the limit may be placed at E♭ or D¹. The lowest which can be taken easily by an average class will be about C.   From this it will be seen that the most suitable keys in which to practise exercises containing upper **d¹** are C, D and E♭, and for **s₁** keys E, F and G.   The key should be changed frequently and **s₁** and **d¹** should not be included in the same key.

RANGE OF VOICE.

DIFFICULT PHRASES. The more difficult intervals should be noted, and one or more introduced into each lesson and practised thoroughly. The following are among the most difficult phrases to be found in the first step :—d¹ s d ; d¹ m s ; d m d¹ ; m d¹ d ; s₁ m s ; s₁ m d ; m s₁ d ; s₁ s d.

THE SECOND STEP. The introduction of the SOH chord will permit of much greater melodic variety than is possible when the tones of the DOH chord alone are available. When the tones are judiciously combined, many beautiful and pleasing melodies can be formed, which will serve to create a renewed interest in the study of the music lesson. Necessarily, new difficulties will also be introduced, but these need not cause any feeling of apprehension, provided the First Step has been thoroughly taught. At each lesson, one of the new tones at least should receive special treatment, in order to establish its mental effect irrespective of the interval by which it may be approached. The following will illustrate the method of "driving home" or "rubbing in," as it is sometimes termed :—Teacher questions regarding the mental effect of **ray**, sings s m s r,

"RUBBING IN" RAY. gives manual sign for **ray** and directs pupils to sing **ray** only whenever the manual sign is given. The teacher will then sing the following, or similar phrases, giving the sign for pupils to sing **ray** after each phrase :—s m d r ; r s r m ; d m r s ; s d¹ s m ; d¹ t d¹ s ; m r d t₁ ; r m d s ; s t t s ; r d t₁ d. By this method pupils will become familiar with **ray** approached from any of the tones already studied.

The next process will be to *imitate* phrases similar to the above, singing **ray** from the manual sign after each phrase, thus :—Teacher sings **r m d s,** pupils imitate ; teacher gives sign for **ray,** pupils sing **ray.** When this has been sufficiently practised, pupils will be prepared to sing exercises of moderate difficulty from the modulator.   At first it is advisable to return to the new tone frequently, pausing slightly or repeating the tone to allow its effect to be clearly felt.

EXAMPLE :—

KEYS C, D.

|d m d s |r — m d |r — s m |d — r — |m s r r

|d r r t, |r r s m |r — — — |m d r — |s m r —

|s d' t d' |s r r — |d m r — |r m d t, |d r t, d |r r d —

The same method applies to the teaching of **te,** the manual signs, etc., being first given, then modulator exercises with **te** predominating.   It will be noticed that the singing of **te** will unconsciously lead to the anticipation of the **doh** above.   This *leading* tendency is found in other tones of the scale, but is

LEADING TONE.

most strongly felt in **te.**   From this peculiar characteristic **te** has been termed the " *leading tone* " of the scale.   The ear cannot be satisfied with a tune or phrase which ends on **te.**   In order to satisfy the ear, and secure a feeling of completeness at the close of a phrase, **te** should invariably be followed by the **doh** immediately above. This leading tendency must not, however, be too freely indulged in throughout the exercises, as the thing to be taught is not *how* to sing **t d¹**, but how to prevent its being sung when another interval is required. The best means of accomplishing this will be found in dwelling on the SOH chord. This makes the singing of **s t r¹** as simple as **d ᴍ s**, the intervals being exactly similar.

EXAMPLE :—

KEY C.

d	ᴍ	d	s	s	s	r	r	s	t	r¹	t	t	r¹	s	—
t	t	s	t	d¹	t	d¹	r¹	t	r¹	r¹	d¹	t	—	d¹	—
d¹	s	ᴍ	s	s	r	t₁	r	t₁	d	r	t₁	d	ᴍ	r	—
r	s	t	s	s	r	t₁	r	d	ᴍ	r	t₁	d	—	—	—

The following are a few of the more difficult phrases to be found in the second step, for subsequent practice :

s ᴍ r, ᴍ s t, t ᴍ, t₁ ᴍ, ᴍ t, s t₁, d¹ r, ᴍ r d¹, r t, t r, d t d¹.

SIGHT-SINGING.

FIRST STEP. In teaching Sight-Singing the same difficulties have to be met as in Modulator Drill. At each lesson, one or more of the difficult intervals of the step should be introduced and practised thoroughly. The following exercises must be preceded by the exercises on **d ᴍ s** and the lesson on Octaves :—

Keys C, D, E♭. Range d to d¹.

d s m s d¹ d¹ s m s d s m d

m m d s m d¹ m̈ s d̈ d¹ s m d

d m d s m d¹ d̈ m s m s s d

s d¹ s m d' s d̈ m d s d¹ s m

d¹ s m m d̈' d̈ s s d¹ s m s d¹

m d̈ s m d¹ ṅ d s d¹ m̈ s s d¹

Keys E♭, E, F, G. Range s₁ to s.

d m d s₁ d s₁ d m s m s s̈₁ d

m d s₁ s₁ d s₁ d m r s̈₁ m̈ m d

d m s s̈₁ d s₁ d s̈ m m s̈₁ m d

d s₁ d m s₁ s₁ d m s̈₁ m̈ s s₁ d

The * denotes the points of difficulty.

Exercises containing several varieties of tune may now be combined under one rhythmic form.

Ex. 1. Keys C, D, E♭. Range d to d¹.

a. |d :m |s :— |d¹ :s |m :— ‖

b. |m :s |d¹ :— |m :d |s¹ :— ‖

c |s :m |d¹ :— |d¹ :s |d¹ :— ‖

d. |m :s |d¹ :— |d¹ :m |s :— ‖

e. |d :d¹ |s :— |m :d¹ |d :— ‖

Ex. 2. KEYS E♭, E, F, G. RANGE s₁ TO s.

a. :d ! s₁ | :s₁.s₁ | d :m | s :s.s | d ‖

b. :s₁ | d :d.d | m :d | s :m.m | d ‖

c. :m | d :d.m | s :m | s :s.m | d ‖

d. :d | m :s.m | d :s₁ | d :m.s | d ‖

e. :m | s :m.d | s :m | s :m.s | d ‖

SECOND STEP.

In this step the same methods will be adopted as in the previous step, the exercises being preceded by modulator drill on the new tones **te** and **ray**.

KEYS C, D. RANGE t₁ TO r¹.

d m s s s t r¹ t d¹ s m r d

s m r s r m d r t₁ d s r d

d s m s r s d t₁ d s r t₁ d

m d r r t₁ r s — s r t₁ r d

KEYS E♭, E, F, G. RANGE s₁ TO s.

d t₁ d s₁ d r t₁ d s r m s d

m d s s₁ d t₁ r d s t₁ d r m

KEYS G, A, B♭. RANGE m₁ TO m.

d s₁ m₁ s₁ d t₁ d s₁ t₁ r s₁ t₁ d

s₁ d t₁ d r t₁ s₁ d m₁ m₁ s₁ s₁ d

d m d s₁ m r d s₁ r m r t₁ d

Keys E♭ to G.　Range s₁ to s.

a. :d₁ |m　:r .r |d　:s　|d　:t₁.t₁ |d　‖

b. :m |d　:t₁.d |r　:t₁　|d　:s₁.s₁ |d　‖

c. :d |s　:m.r |d　:r　|s₁　:d.t₁ |d　‖

d. :s |m　:d.r |m　:d　|r　:m.r |d　‖

| Tones Represented by Colors. |

Among those who have investigated the matter, there can be no doubt regarding the advantage to be derived from the use of colors in teaching sight-singing. The object of a color-scale should be to convey, through the eye to the mind, a distinct impression of the effect of the tones represented. We have discussed the appropriateness of certain colors, with a large number of artists and teachers, and, as a result, have decided to adopt the following scale :—

t—Purple.
l—Indigo.
s—Yellow.
f—Green.
m—Blue.
r—Orange.
d—Red.

It will be noticed that the prismatic colors have been selected, with a slight modification of their natural order. Some writers have advocated the retaining of the natural order, but we cannot reconcile the calm, gentle effect of **me** with the brightness of yellow ; or the bright, bold effect of **soh** with the peaceful effect of blue. In practice it is not advisable to write all the tones by means of colors, but only those which occasion a difficulty in singing.

EXAMPLE :—

d m d s d¹ m̊ s d.

COMPARISON OF COLORS. Suppose the above exercise written with ordinary white crayon on the blackboard, and pupils have made the mistake of singing **s** instead of **m̊**. Let each **m** be written with *blue* crayon, and pupils led to notice the oneness of color and the oneness of sound. When the second **m** is reached the color will recall the impression of the first, and almost invariably will lead to its being **CONTRAST OF COLORS.** correctly sung. The same result may be obtained by contrasting **s** with **m**. Let **s** be written with yellow, and **m** with blue. Contrast the colors, and show pupils that they have actually been singing the same sound for the blue note as for the yellow. They will thus be put on their guard, and will not be liable to sing the same sound for two notes differing so widely in appearance. The same methods will apply to all other tones.

TIME.

When pupils have been well drilled in exercises containing whole-pulse tones and continued tones, and have received the first lesson in divided pulses, exercises containing divided pulses should be freely introduced. These will at first be taught on one tone only, but should be combined with melody as soon as practicable. The simplest form of melody is that in which the same note appears in each half of the divided pulse, as :—

$$|d \quad .d \quad || \qquad |m \quad .m \quad |$$

In blackboard exercises it will be found advantageous

COLOR IN PULSES.

to use colored crayons for writing the *pulse-signs.* One uniform color should be used for all pulse-signs—strong, weak and medium. This directs the eye to the signs which represent the pulsations or beats which are felt in singing, and materially assists in overcoming the common tendency to give a full beat to each tone. The half-pulse sign (.) may be colored, but must be of a different color from the pulse-signs. The hints given on page 82 will apply equally to the following exercises. See also "Time," pages 17 and 31.

Ex. 1.   Keys D to A.

a. |d   :r.r|m   :r.r|d   :t₁.t₁|d   :— |

b. |d   :r.r|m   :r |d.d:t₁.t₁|d   :— |

c. |d   :r |m.m:r |d.d:t₁ |d   :— |

d. |d   :r.r|m.m:r |d   :t₁.t₁|d   :— |

e. |d.d:r |m.m:r |d.d:t₁ |d   :— |

f. |d.d:r.r|m.m:r.r|d   :t₁.t₁|d   :— |

g. |d.d:r.r|m.m:r.r|d   :t₁.t₁|d   :— |

Ex. 2. SAME KEYS AS ABOVE.

a. | d :d.d :r.r | m :m :r.r | d :t₁ :t₁.t₁ | d :— :— ||

b. | d :d.d :r | m :m.m :r | d :t₁.t₁ :t₁ | d :— :— ||

c. | d :d :r.r | m.m :m :r.r | d :t₁ :t₁.t₁ | d :— :— ||

d. | d :d :r.r | m.m :m :r.r | d :t₁.t₁ :t₁ | d :— :— ||

e. | d :— :r.r | m :— :r.r | d :— :t₁.t₁ | d :— :— ||

Ex. 3. SAME KEYS AS ABOVE. (With change of tones).

a. | d :d . r | m :— | m :m . r | d :— ||

b. | d :d . r | m :m . r | d :d . t₁ | d :— ||

c. | d . r :m | r :— | r . d :t₁ | d :— ||

d. | d :r | m . r :d | m.r :d . t₁ | d :— ||

e. | d.t₁ :d . r | m :— | r . d :t₁ | d :— ||

Any of the above exercises may be converted into secondary form, by commencing on the weak pulse and deducting one pulse from the last note in order to equalise the form, thus :—

:d | d :r.r | m :r.r | d :t₁.t₁ | d ||

SIX-PULSE MEASURE. Ordinary six-pulse measure may be taught by the same method as three-pulse measure. At this stage quick six-pulse

measure (see page 40) may be introduced with advantage. Its lively rhythm will tend to brighten the
exercises and songs, and will add much to the pleasure
of the music-lesson. The Time-names for thirds of a
pulse will be rather confusing for the pupils of this
grade, and should be deferred till later. The most
suitable plan will be to teach the exercises as in
ordinary six-pulse measure, and then gradually increase the speed and beat twice in measure Pupils
will readily perceive that the beats occur on the strong
and medium accents only.

Ex. 4. SAME KEYS AS ABOVE.

|d :t₁ :d |r :d :r |m :r :m |d :— :— ||

|d :t₁ :d |r :— :— |r :d :r |m :— :— ||

|d :t₁ :d.d|r :d :r.r|m :m :r.r|d :— :— ||

|d.d:t₁ :d |r.r:d :r |m.m:r :m |d :— :— ||

|d :d :t₁.d|r :r :d.r|m :m :m.r|d :— :— ||

DICTATION. In addition to the above, exercises
in writing from dictation should frequently be given. These will assist in training the
eye to read the notation of time. The primary
exercises should consist of writing measures only,
thus :—Teacher will direct pupils to write two two-
pulse measures, explaining the relative length of the
bar and colon. (See page 36.) Three and four-pulse
measure may then be dictated. The next process

will consist of writing notes of various lengths, thus :—
Teacher directs pupils to write two four-pulse measures, then dictates slowly :-—First pulse **doh** ; second
pulse, **ray** ; third, **me** ; fourth, **ray**, with *Taa-tai*, etc.
When all have finished, the slates may be examined,
and the more common mistakes pointed out and
corrected by judicious questioning.   When pupils
succeed in writing an exercise fairly well, they should
be rewarded by being allowed to sing from their own
written copy.   This is usually considered a reward
worthy of their best efforts.

EAR EXERCISES.

In conducting ear exercises, the teacher should
carefully avoid taking answers from the few sharp
pupils only, but should endeavour to make the exer-
| IMITATION EXERCISES. | cises so simple and interesting that
all will be able to take part.   The
simplest exercises for training young pupils to listen
well are those in which the teacher sol-fas a short
phrase to which the pupils listen, and afterwards
imitate.   These should consist only of the tones
which have been studied.

EXAMPLES :—

FIRST STEP.

d	m	d	s		s	m	s	d		m	s	d	m	
s	m	d	s₁		s₁	d	s₁	m		s	d¹	s	d	
m	d	s	m		s	d¹	m	s		d¹	s	m	d¹	
d	s₁	m	d		m	d	s	d		s	d	s	m	

SECOND STEP.

| d | m | d | r | ‖ | r | s | r | m | ‖ | d | r | t₁ | d | ‖ |

| r | s | r | t₁ | ‖ | r | s | t₁ | d | ‖ | d | t₁ | r | d | ‖ |

| m | r | s | d | ‖ | d | s₁ | t₁ | r | ‖ | r | s | m | r | ‖ |

| s | t | s | d¹ | ‖ | d¹ | t | d¹ | s | ‖ | d¹ | s | m | r | ‖ |

| d¹ | t | s | d¹ | ‖ | m | d¹ | s | t | ‖ | d¹ | m | r | d | ‖ |

Variety of rhythm may be introduced with advantage as it helps to make the exercises more interesting and lively.

EXAMPLES :—

| d | :d.d | m | :— | ‖ | | d | :m.d | s | :— | ‖ |

| s | :d¹ | t.d¹:s | ‖ | | m | :s | r.m:d | ‖ |

| m.r:d | r | :— | ‖ | | s.m:d | s | :— | ‖ |

| :s₁ | d | :m.r | d | ‖ | :s₁ | r | :d.r | m | ‖ |

In all the above the key must be adapted to the compass of the voices. The next method is that in which the attention is concentrated on one particular tone surrounded by several others.

EXAMPLE OF METHOD.

Teacher.—Can you tell me what kind of tone **doh** is ?
Class.—Strong and firm.

Teacher.—I am going to sing several tones, and I want you to listen very carefully, and tell me which one sounds like **doh**.

| FINDING DOH. |
(Writes on blackboard 1, 2, 3, 4, gives the key-tone, then sings s m s d to *laa* while pointing to the numerals.) Raise hands all who can tell me on which number I sang **doh**. Tommy will come up and point it out. (Pupil points number two.)

Teacher.—I will sing it again, and you will listen and find out whether that one is firm enough for **doh**. (Repeats with soft emphasis on **me** and strong on **doh**.) Now, what do you think of number two?

Class.—It was not firm enough for **doh**.

Teacher.—Quite right; but where was **doh**? Those who think it was on number one, raise hands, on three, on four. I see you all now think it was on four, that is correct. You will now try and find **doh** again, and will write what you think is the correct number on your slates. (Sings m d s m to *laa*, while pupils listen and write.) Those who have number one will raise hands; number two; three; four. Number two is correct.

The act of writing the answers compels each pupil to think for himself, and is a sure means of ascertain-

| WRITING IN EAR EXERCISES. |
ing whether they are equal to the exercises. With very young pupils it is advisable to use some well-known objects in place of the numerals. Four little boys may be brought to the front, or an equal number of birds may be drawn on the blackboard, to which the teacher

| INTERESTING DEVICES. |
may point while singing the exercises. The remaining tones of the step will be treated by the same method as described for **doh**.

After the above have been given it will be an easy matter to concentrate the attention on one particular number, and find out to which tone it is sung. Example.—Write on board 1, 2, 3, *4. Direct pupils to think of four only, and tell to which tone it is sung. Sing **d s d m**, intensifying the mental effect of the fourth tone, and question as above. A number of exercises may be given consecutively and the answers written, and examined at the close. Young pupils will be interested by having a bird drawn in place of number four, and will readily tell which tone the bird sings. In all cases corrections should be made by questioning on the mental effect, but the answer should never be told by the teacher until the pupils have found it for themselves.

Which is **d** ?

s m s d ‖ m d s m ‖ s m d s | d s m m ‖

Which is **s** ?

d m d s ‖ d s d m ‖ d m s d ‖ s m m d ‖

Which is **m** ?

d s d m ‖ d m d s ‖ d s m d ‖ m s s d ‖

Which is **s₁** ?

d m d s₁ ‖ d s₁ d m ‖ m d s₁ d ‖ s₁ d m d ‖

Which is **d¹** ?

d m s d¹ ‖ s m d¹ d ‖ d¹ s m d ‖ s d¹ m s ‖

It is unnecessary to multiply examples here, as any teacher should be able to prepare them without assistance.

Which tone is sung on number four?

FIRST STEP.

| d s m d || d s d m || m s s d || d s m d¹ ||

| m s s d || d m d s || m s d s₁ || s₁ d m d ||

| s d m s₁ || s d s m || m s d¹m || d s s d ||

SECOND STEP.

| d s m r || m r s d || s t s d¹ || d¹ t d¹ s ||

| m s r m || d t₁ d s || s r t₁ d || m d r t₁ ||

| r s t₁ d || m s₁ r d || m r d t₁ || d s₁ t₁ r ||

| s t d¹ r¹ || d¹ t r¹ s || s d¹ r¹ t || s r¹ s m ||

The manual-signs may be used to advantage in the above. EXAMPLE.—Teacher intimates that those who know which tone is sung on a particular number (any number may be taken equally with four) will make

MANUAL-SIGNS IN EAR EXERCISES. its manual-sign and cover it until the command " Hands out," is given. All will then raise hands *instantly without looking at the others*. The teacher will then perceive at a glance how many have the correct answer. Much depends on the simultaneous indication of the manual-signs, as if done slowly copying will certainly be the result. See Ear Cultivation, page 52.

TEACHING SCHOOL SONGS.

Rote songs have been described in a former chapter (page 60). The songs to be taught " by note " at this stage should consist only of the tones and rhythms already studied. The same methods will be employed for teaching the tune as for sight-singing, described above. When the tune has been thoroughly learnt and vocalised, the words should be studied separately, and the thoughts which they contain should form the subject of a " talk " between teacher and pupils. It may, perhaps, be advisable to practice the words and music until they are sung mechanically correct before taking up the subject of expression.

EXAMPLE :—

Morning and Evening.

Key G.   A. T. C.

d :— :d	d :— :d	r :m :r	d :— :s₁
1. When the	ear - - ly	morn is	break - - ing
2. When the	even - - ing	shades are	steal - - ing

r :— :r	r :— :r	r :d :r	m :— :—
In the	east with	gold - - en	ray,
And the	light fades	from the	west,

m :— :m	s :— :m	r :d :r	m :— :d
That's the	time to	be a	wak - - ing
Let a	grate - ful	hymn be	peal - - ing

s :— :m	s :— :m	t₁ :d :r	d :— :—
Songs of	wel - come	to the	day.
For the	night of	qui - - et	rest.

We will suppose that the tune and words of the above song have been sung fairly well, without any special reference having been made to expression. The pupils will now be prepared for a "talk" on the subject in which they will be led to discover whatever beauties the song may contain.

EXAMPLE.

Teacher.—You have sung this song very nicely, but I wonder whether you have been thinking of its meaning. Can you tell me what you have been singing about ?

Class.—About " Morning and Evening."

Teacher.—Quite right. In what part of the song do we sing of morning ?

Class.—In the first verse.

Teacher.—And in what part, of evening ?

Class.—In the second verse.

Teacher.—Let us take the first two lines and think of them only for a little. Can you tell me why morn is spoken of as breaking in the east ?

Class.—It means that the sun rises in the east.

Teacher.—With what kind of ray does the morning break ?

Class.—With golden ray.

Teacher.—If any of you are in the habit of rising in the early morning, you will be able to tell me what a sunrise looks like.

Class.—It is bright. It is beautiful. It is very pretty.

Teacher.—You are all correct. It is one of the grandest sights that anyone can witness. How do you think we should sing of this grand picture ? (No answer.) Do you think we should sing as if we felt sorry that the sun had risen so grand and bright ?

Class.—(Smiling). No ; we should be happy and bright.

Teacher.—Then we must sing that brightly and lively, and when you do so I want you to think of the bright sunrise and imagine that you see it with your eyes. I will watch your faces, and if you really think of what you are singing, I am sure that they will look bright and happy too. (Class sings first two lines with expressive brightness.)

Teacher.—That certainly did sound much better, and you looked much happier also. We will now study the remainder of the verse. At what time are we to be awaking songs of welcome?

Class.—In the early morning.

Teacher.—Yes, that's the time. And what sort of songs are songs of welcome? Do you think we should welcome the day with a careless, lazy kind of song, or a bright, hearty song?

Class.—With a bright, hearty song.

Teacher.—You will now sing the whole verse, and you must sing as if you were really giving a hearty welcome to something which you are pleased to have.

This will be followed by a similar "talk" on the second verse, in which the characteristics of evening, the twilight fading in the west, and the hymn of gratitude and prayer for quiet repose are contrasted with the brightness and light-heartedness of the morning.

The above method may be considered tedious and unnecessary. Some teachers may consider it quite sufficient to *tell* the pupils to sing the first verse

| MECHANICAL EXPRESSION. |

lively, or loudly, and the second softly. This would certainly result in the song being sung with a certain degree of expression, but it could only be of a mechanical, unintelligent description, productive of no educational advantage. Its importance cannot be too strongly urged upon the teacher. If pupils are trained to think intelligently of what they sing at this early stage, the practice of "singing with the heart and not with the lips only" will become a confirmed habit, and in a short time they will learn to investigate for themselves and discover new beauties in all they undertake. This will surely recompense the thoughtful teacher for the care bestowed upon the subject during the few minutes occupied in teaching the lesson. Dr. Arnold once

> **"LEARNING HOW."**

said to his pupils, " You come here, not to read, but to *learn how to read.*" This principle of " *learning how* " should unfailingly be applied in teaching how to sing with the understanding.

VOICE-TRAINING.

During this stage no elaborate exercises for voice-training are necessary ; in fact, one simple chordal exercise is sufficient for all practical purposes. All exercises should be sung with a soft, pure quality of tone. Attention should be given principally to the formation of correct methods in singing, and the eradication of whatever faulty habits may have already been formed. The tone should be delivered with precision and thrown well forward in the mouth. For this purpose, syllables composed of the consonant *k* and the various vowels will be found most useful. The mouth should be opened widely. The vowel *ah* is the most useful for this purpose. *Ai* and *ee* should at first be avoided on account of the tendency to sing them with the mouth almost closed.

EXAMPLE :—

|d :m |s :m |d :— |— : ||

Exercises in " Attack."	Koo koo koo koo koo...............
	Ko ko ko ko ko ....
	Kaa kaa kaa kaa kaa................
Resonance.	Scah ....
	Oh ....
	Oo ....
	Oo oh ah oh oo ....

The preceding may be commenced in the key of C and gradually raised to A,, provided proper care is taken to prevent forcing of voice. If the exercise is *softly* sung no danger need be feared, as the registers will take care of themselves naturally. In the last form of the exercise the forward delivery of tone which naturally accompanies the vowel *oo* must be retained in singing *oh* and *ah*, the shape of the mouth being gradually altered for each vowel.

CHAPTER XII.

NOTES ON DIVISION II.

LESSON ON THIRD STEP.

PREPARE blackboard by writing diagram of second step modulator, leaving space between **m** and **s**, and **s** and **t**. Drill class in singing from modulator. Give ear exercises in which pupils anticipate a new tone. Which tone is sung on No. 4. Teacher singing to *laa* ‖ d m d s ‖ d m d r ‖ d s d m ‖ d m d f* ‖ The three first exercises will prepare for the fourth, in which the new tone will be discovered at once.

m¹
r¹
d¹
t
s
m
r
d

Teacher.—Which tone did you hear on No. 4?

Class.—A new tone.

Teacher.—I will sing the same phrase again, and you will sing it after me. (Repeats phrase, class imitate.) At what place in the scale shall we place the new tone?

Class.—Between **m** and **s**.

Teacher—Quite correct. The name of the new tone is **fah.** (Writes it in position.) Now sing from my pointing. (Points

d s d m d d d f f f m.) You seem to have a little difficulty in singing **fah**, but you will find it much easier when you have studied its mental effect. Listen while I sing, and tell me what you think of the character of **fah**. (Sings several phrases in which **fah** is made prominent.)

Class.—It has a *dull* sound ; it is solemn ; it is gloomy. (Such answers may not be given at first, but a repetition of the exercises will elicit them readily. The writer has received as many as sixteen different answers to this question, all tending to show that pupils had grasped the idea of the mental effect of the new tone.)

Teacher.—There seems to be a difference of opinion regarding the character of **fah**. Let me try to help you. Just suppose that you are at play in the yard, when a boy comes up to one of you and tells you that there is a policeman in the schoolroom wishing to speak to you. How do you think you would feel about it ?

Class.—We would feel rather serious.

Teacher.—But suppose this same boy should run up to you and tell you that " Teacher says you are to have a half-holiday," how would you feel about it ?

Class.—We would feel happy.

Teacher.—Now that you see the difference between these two situations, perhaps you will be able to tell me which one **fah** most resembles.

Class.—The serious one.

Teacher.—Yes, **fah** is really a very serious, gloomy tone. Now practise singing from the modulator, and think of the effect of **fah** each time you sing it.

As soon as possible after **fah** has been taught, **lah** should be introduced, as **fah** is more easily sung when in connection with **lah** and **doh**. The same method as above will be used, being careful to approach **lah** from **fah**, thus : ‖ d f f s ‖ d f f l ‖ The mental effect of **lah** is sad and plaintive.

Great care must be taken to impress the difference in the mental effect of the tones **fah** and **lah**, as they resemble each other to a certain extent.

Pupils should not be kept too long on this lesson, as the mental effect of the new tones is so depressing that they will quickly become dull and even unable to respond readily to your questioning. The introduction of some bright song, previously learnt, will serve to counteract the depression.

MODULATOR DRILL.

The introduction of **fah** and **lah** completes the scale and permits of an almost endless variety of melodic combinations. As in the previous steps, the new tones should receive special attention until their mental effect has been firmly established. Owing to the marked leading tendency of **fah** towards **me** there is always a danger of flattening in pitch when practising the new tones. This must be guarded against from the outset, as the habit once formed is exceedingly difficult to rectify. The effect of **fah** and **lah** can be more clearly impressed when contrasted with the brighter tones of the scale, as :— d m d *s || d m d *f || s d' t *d' || s d' t *l | d' t d' *s || d' t d' *l || In Division II. simple exercises only are given, the more difficult intervals being reserved for Division III. The method described on page 90 should be employed in modulator drill at this stage.

THIRD STEP
MODULATOR.

f'
m'
r'
DOH'
TE
LAH
SOH
FAH
ME
RAY
DOH
t,
l,
s,
f,
m,

SIGHT-SINGING.

During this stage the teacher may unconsciously introduce unnecessarily difficult intervals, unless the lessons have been previously prepared. The simplest form of approach to the tones **f** or **l** is from the tones of the FAH chord, thus :—**d m s d f l d¹ l f m r r d.** The following rule will serve as a guide in composing exercises for sight-singing. Approach **f** and **l** by chordal leap, or by step, from the tones immediately above or below, all other tones may be approached by leap.

EXERCISES. KEYS C TO E♭. COMPASS t₁ TO d¹.

d	m	d	s	m	f	l	d¹	l	f	m	f	r	d
d	s	m	f	r	m	f	s	l	s	d¹	l	t	d¹
m	d	f	r	s	m	f	f	s	l	s	l	s	d
s	d	r	t₁	d	m	f	r	s	l	f	l	t	d¹
d	m	f	s	s	l	l	s	d¹	l	f	s	f	m
d¹	t	l	s	d¹	t	d¹	l	l	f	r	l	l	s

Exercises in which the tones move by step followed by a sudden leap occasion a slight difficulty. They are useful in checking the tendency to anticipate, and in cultivating close attention.

EXERCISE 1. KEY C.

d r m f s d¹ t l s m r d t₁ d

EXERCISE 2. KEY F.

m d r s f m r t₁ d r t₁ d r d

EXERCISE 3. KEY G.

d t₁ l₁ t₁ d r m s f m r d l₁ d

EXERCISE 4. KEY G.

m d f m r d l₁ s₁ l₁ t₁ r d t₁ d

EXERCISE 5. KEY A.

d t₁ d s₁ f₁ m₁ f₁ s₁ t₁ r t₁ d s₁ m₁

EXERCISE 6. KEY B♭.

d s₁ m₁ d₁ f₁ s₁ l₁ t₁ d f r d s₁ d

The methods of employing rhythmic exercises, and colors, described in the previous chapter, apply equally to this step.

TIME.

LESSON ON HALF-PULSE CONTINUATIONS.

Prepare blackboard with two four-pulse measures.

|d :r |m :m.r|d :d.t₁|d :— ||

| REVIEW. | *Teacher.*—You have already learned how to sing whole-pulse tones, half-pulse tones, and prolonged tones, and to-day we will study some |

new combinations in rhythm. In this exercise, can you tell me how many tones we have which are only one pulse long?

Class.—Four.

Teacher.—How many are two pulses long?

Class.—One.

Teacher.—And how many pulses are divided into halves?

Class.—Two.

Teacher.—Now tell me the time-names for each pulse as I point to it.

| INTRODUCTION OF AA TAI. | *Class.*—Taa, Taa, Taa, Taa-tai, Taa, Taa-tai, Taa-aa. |

Teacher.—You will now sing the time-names as I point. (Class sings as desired.) Now sing to *laa* while I beat time. (Class sings as desired.) You can sing that correctly, and will now be able to tell whether I sing it without any mistake. (Sings it correctly to *laa* while pupils listen.) Did I make any mistake?

Class.—No.

Teacher.—Listen once more. (Sings as before, prolonging third tone half-way through fourth pulse.) Did you notice any mistake?

Class.—Yes.

Teacher.—In which pulse was the mistake made?

Class.—In the fourth pulse.

Teacher.—Did I sing both of the tones in the fourth pulse?

Class.—No; you omitted the first one.

Teacher.—I did omit the first one; but, can you tell me whether I sang anything in its place?

Class.—You continued the third tone into the fourth pulse.

Teacher.—Quite right. The time-name for this rhythm is **taa-aa-tai.** Please sing it after me. (Gives pattern, **taa-aa-tai,** and class sing it repeatedly, in order to catch the effect of the new rhythm.) You can now sing that nicely and I think will be able to tell me how to write its notation. We will rub out the first note in the fourth pulse. What sign do we use to express a continued tone?

Class.—A dash.

Teacher.—Yes; we usually have a long dash for the continuation through a full pulse, but as this tone has only to be continued through half a pulse we will use a short dash. (Writes |**d :-.d**|.) You will now see how we get the time-names for this rhythm. What is the time-name for the third pulse note?

Class.—**Taa.**

Teacher.—For the continuation?

Class.—**Aa.**

Teacher.—And for the last half of a pulse?

Class.—**Tai.**

(Writes from pupils' dictation |**d :– .d**|
Taa - aa- Tai.)

Teacher.—We will now practise singing this new rhythm in tune. Please sing it to the time-names; now to the syllables on one tone. (In the latter, pupils

| SINGING IN TUNE. |

will probably fail. Some will sing **ray** at fourth beat instead of continuing **me.** This may be overcome by slightly accenting the continuation at fourth pulse, or by using colored crayons as follows:—Teacher writes the **m** and the dash in *blue,* and the **r** in *orange.*) What is the color of **m**? Of the dash?

Class.—Blue.

Teacher.—If both are of the same *color*, does it not indicate that they should have the same *sound* ?

Class.—Yes ; they should be the same.

Teacher.—Is **r** of the same color as the others ?

Class.—No ; it is orange.

Teacher.—Then if the color is changed we should certainly change the sound. Does the color change at the beginning of the pulse or at the middle ?

Class.—At the middle.

Teacher.—Then you must be careful not to sing **ray** at the beginning of the pulse, but to prolong **me** half-way through, and then sing **ray**.

When the exercise has been correctly sung it should be followed by ear exercises in which the teacher sings phrases of several measures in length while the pupils listen for the new rhythm, and tell the number of times it occurs in each phrase.

PRACTICE.

In practice it will be found necessary to employ various means of securing correctness in singing the new rhythm. The color method will be found the most useful for training the eye. This may be supplemented by the emphasizing of the prolongation of the vowel sound, thus :—

$$\left|\begin{matrix} m \\ Me \end{matrix}\ \ :\!-\!.r\ \begin{matrix} e \end{matrix}\right.\left|\begin{matrix} d \\ Doh \end{matrix}\ :\!-\!.m\ \begin{matrix} oh \end{matrix}\right|\begin{matrix} s \\ Soh \end{matrix}\ :\!-\!.f\ \begin{matrix} oh \end{matrix}\left|\begin{matrix} m \end{matrix}\ :\!-\ \right|\!\right|$$

It should also be pointed out that the ear naturally expects the last half of the pulse to lead and connect with the pulse which follows.

Ex. i.   KEYS D TO A.

a. | d   :d .r | m   :—.r | d   :d .t₁ | d   :— ||

b. | d   :—.r | m   :—.r | d   :d .t₁ | d   :— ||

c. | d :—.r | m :m .r | d :d .t, | d :— ‖

d. | d :—.r | m :—.r | d :—.t, | d :— ‖

e. | d :—.r | m :m .r | d :—.t, | d :— ‖

A fresh difficulty will be experienced when *-aa Tai* is immediately followed by *Taa-Tai.*

Ex. 2. SAME KEYS AS ABOVE

a. | d :—.r | m :—.f | s .f :m .r | d :— ‖

b. | d :—.r | m .f :s | f :m .r | d :— ‖

c. | d .r :m .f | s :—.f | m :m .r | d :— ‖

d. | d .r :m | f :—.s | f :m .r | d :— ‖

e. | d .r :m | — :—.f | s .f :m .r | d :— ‖

-Aa-Tai is exceptionally difficult when it occurs in three-pulse measure. The most common error is to substitute a full-pulse continuation followed by half-pulses.

Ex. 3. KEYS C OR D.

a. | d :r :m | f :—.s :l | t :— :t | d¹ :— :— ‖

b. | d :— :r | m :—.f :s | l :— :t | d¹ :— :— ‖

c. | d :—.r :m | f :— :— | s :—.l :t | d¹ :— :— ‖

d. | d :— :— | r :—.m:f | s :—.l :t | d¹ :— :— ‖

e. | d :—.r :m | f :—.s :l | t :—.t :t | d¹ :— :— ‖

The preceding may be converted into secondary measure by commencing on the weak accent, and deducting one pulse from the length of the last note.

SILENT PULSES. (RESTS.)

In teaching a first lesson on *silent* pulses, the same methods as described in the foregoing specimen lessons may be adopted, viz.:—The new rhythm introduced in ear exercises by the teacher, detected and imitated by the pupils, and developed by appropriate interrogation. Theoretically, it seems an anomaly to use a time-name to express a silence, but, practically, it will be found exceedingly valuable. The sensation of pulses in music is so powerful that unless something is provided to be sung on the stroke of the silent pulse, untrained pupils will invariably sing the succeeding tone. The act of *whispering* the time-name involves a certain degree of restraint which compels the singer to observe the silence when singing in tune. The pupils should at first sing *all* the time-names, then the teacher may sing those for the silent pulses, and finally the pupils will sing all but the silent pulses, merely *thinking* the time-names as they occur in the exercise.

Ex. 4. KEYS C TO A.

a. |d :r |m : |f :m.r |d :— ||

b. |d.r :m | :f.m |r : |d :— ||

c. |d : |r.m :f.m |r : |d :— ||

d. | d :r | :m | f :m .r | d :— ‖

e. | d :— .r | m :f .m | r : | d :— ‖

Ex. 5. KEYS C OR D.

a. | d : :r | m : :f | s :l :t | d¹ :— :— ‖

b. | d :r : | m :f : | s :l :t | d¹ :— :— ‖

c. | d : :r | m :f :s | l :t : | d¹ :— : ‖

d. | d :r : | :m :f | s :l :t | d¹ :— :— ‖

e. | d :r :m | :f :s | l : :t | d¹ :— :— ‖

EAR EXERCISES.

These will be conducted by exactly the same methods as prescribed for Division I. Care must be observed in impressing the mental effects of **f, l** and **m**, as, owing to their seeming resemblance, one is frequently mistaken for the other. This difficulty may readily be overcome by frequent comparison of the tones, as :— **d s d *m ‖ d s d *f ‖ d s d *l ‖ d¹ s d¹ *l ‖ d¹ s d¹ *m ‖ d¹ s d¹ f ‖**

Exercises in finding **fah** :—

1	2	3	4	5
d	t₁	d	f	m
m	d	l	f	s
d	f	r	s	d
s	m	l	s	f

1	2	3	4	5
s	d	f	r	d
s	l	s	f	m
d	t₁	d	m	f
d	f	r	m	d

Exercises in finding **lah** :—

I	2	3	4	5
s	d¹	t	d¹	l
d	f	r	l	s
m	s	l	f	s
d	f	r	f	l

I	2	3	4	5
d	s	m	l	s
d¹	l	s	f	m
s	d¹	t	l	s
d¹	s	l	t	d¹

Exercises on all tones of the scale.   Which is last ?

I	2	3	4	5
d	s	d	m	r
d¹	t	d¹	s	l
m	d	f	r	s
s	l	f	s	m

I	2	3	4	5
s	m	f	r	d
d	s	l	t	d¹
d¹	m	l	l	t
s	l	s	m	f

The above will be followed by exercises in naming any one tone sung to *ah* or *oh*.   The teacher will *sol-fa* the chord **d¹ s m d**, then sing to *ah* or *oh* any one tone.   Pupils will then give the sol-fa name of the tone.

PREPARED SONG.

This will be taught in the manner described for Div. I.   See pages 57 and 106.

CHAPTER XIII.

NOTES ON DIVISION III.

MODULATOR DRILL.

IN this Division pupils are expected to sing any tones of the scale, irrespective of the interval by which they may be approached. The simpler intervals having been taught in the preceding division, the more difficult intervals will now demand attention. The intervals which usually occasion the most trouble are sixths, as **d l, l, f, t r,** and fourths, as **f d, m t,, m l.** When two such intervals are given in succession, as **s, d f, r s d',** the difficulty is considerably increased. The following are a few of the more difficult intervals included in this step :—**m l, l m, d f, d l, l r', l, r, r' l, m t,, t, m, t, f, f t, r t, t r, l d, f l,, l, f.**

In every lesson one or more of the above should be specially taught, but should be intermingled with simpler intervals in order that the pupils may not be discouraged by too many difficulties. The method described on page 78 for teaching **soh** should be freely employed in teaching **fah** and **lah.**

Examples of exercises for Modulator Drill and Sight-Singing :

KEY C.

d m s d' t l l s f l f m m l l m r r l f r d t, d

s d' t l d' l l d' r' r' l r' m' l l s l f l f r l t d'

d s f f m r f m d f s l f l t t f t d' f m f r d

d f m l f f s l f d' f m d f r f m r f d f r t, d

Key E.

d s l m f r s d¹ f m r l t l s d¹ t l f r d t₁ d

Key A.

d s₁ m₁ s₁ l₁ f₁ s₁ d r f m d l₁ t₁ s₁ d f₁ m₁ l₁ s₁ d t₁ d

Key F.

d t₁ d s₁ l₁ d f m l f s m f r t₁ d s m l f s r d

SIGHT-SINGING FROM BOOKS.

When music books are introduced into the school-room for the first time, teachers are frequently surprised at the difficulty which pupils experience in singing exercises less difficult than many which they have previously sung from the blackboard. The explanation is simple. In blackboard exercises the teacher usually points to each pulse as it is sung, consequently every eye is concentrated on a particular point, and "losing the place" is an impossibility; but when books are used pupils have to find each pulse for themselves, hence the confusion which usu-

EYE TRAINING.

ally results. At this stage special gymnastics in "eye training" should be given, both from blackboard and books, and the practice of pointing to the pulse signs should, be discontinued.

EXAMPLE OF METHOD.

Write on the blackboard an exercise containing continued tones and divided pulses, as :—

|d :m |s :m.d |r :d.t₁ |d :— }

|s :— |m :d.r |m :r.r |d :— ‖

Teacher.—I will now tap the pulses of this tune, and you will watch each pulse as I tap. Should I stop before reaching the end you will show me on which pulse I stop. (Taps audibly without pointing to the pulses, ending on the seventh pulse.) Tell me on which pulse I finished.

Class.—On the *second* pulse of the second measure.

Teacher.—Will someone point to the last pulse that was tapped? (Pupil points to d in the pulse previous to the correct one.) No doubt you think that is the correct pulse, but you have been watching *notes*, not *pulses*. Try once more and watch the pulses only, no matter how many notes they may contain.

This will invariably lead to correct answers being given. The same method should be followed with simple exercises in printed books, or the teacher may sing the exercise to *laa* while pupils *point to each pulse*. When the teacher stops singing, each pupil should be able to point to the exact pulse on which the pause is made. Exercises containing full-pulse tones only should be used at first, and gradually increased in difficulty until the books can be used with the same freedom as the blackboard.

TIME.

The division of the pulse into quarters may be taught by the methods described on page 86 for half-pulses. No difficulty need be experienced when singing on one tone; but when singing in tune is attempted, there will be a decided inclination to slacken the *tempo* whenever quarter-pulses make their appearance. This may be overcome by *sol-faing* on one tone previous to singing in tune, and also by directing pupils to aim at singing in strict time the *first note* of the pulse which follows the divided pulse. If this habit is once formed the divided pulses will soon be found to take care of themselves.

Exercises in quarter pulses :

a.

|d :r .r |m :r,r.r,r|d :t, .t, |d :— ||

b.

|d :r,r.r ,r|m :r .r |d :t,,t,.t,,t,|d : ||

c.

|d :r,r .r,r|m :r |d,d.d,d:t, .t, |d :— ||

d.

|d :r |m,m.m,m:r .r |d :t,,t,.t,,t,|d :— ||

e

|d :r .r |m,m.m,m:r |d,d.d,d:t, .t, |d :— ||

With change of tone :—

|d :r .r |m :f |s :s,f.m,r|d :— ||

|d :d,r.m,f |s :— |s :s,f.m,r|d :— ||

|d :d,r.m,f |s :s,f.m,r|d :t, .t, |d :— ||

|d :d,r.m,f |s :— |s,f.m,r:d .t, |d :— ||

|d :— |d,r.m,f :s,f.m,r|d :t, |d :— ||

EAR EXERCISES.

The first class of ear exercises prescribed for Div. III. are similar to those prescribed for Div. II.

The second class comprise the simplest form of exercises containing more than one tone. In preparing for those exercises it must be made clear to the

pupils that only three tones in stepwise order will be
given. They may also be required to name three
such tones, beginning with any tone indicated by the
teacher, thus :—Name three tones ascending in stepwise order from **d** ; descending from **s** ; ascending
from **l**, etc. The teacher may now sing several such
phrases to *laa*, pupils being required to tell only
whether the phrase ascends or descends. This should
be followed by similar phrases in which they are
required simply to name the first tone. When they
have learned to distinguish between ascending and
descending phrases, and to concentrate their attention
on the first tone, there should not be much difficulty
experienced in naming any of the phrases required.
Previous to singing each phrase, the teacher must
sol-fa the DOH chord, in order to clearly define the
key. When incorrect answers are given, the attention
should be directed to the mental effect of the first
tone, and pupils questioned regarding its resemblance
to the corresponding tone of the correct answer.
When this has been discovered by the majority of the
pupils the exercise should be sol-faed by all   It will
be noticed that exercises which begin with **d, m** or **s**
will be more easily named than those which begin
with the other tones of the scale.

d	r	m	m	r	d	d	t,	l,	s	f	m	s	l	t
d'	t	l	d'	r'	m'	m	f	s	f	m	r	r	m	f
r	d	t,	f	s	l	l	s	f	l	t	d'	t	l	s
t,	d	r	s,	l,	t,	l,	t,	d	r'	d'	t	t,	l,	s,

Exercises in which the tones move by step, but not continuously in one direction, may now be given.

d	t₁	d	d	r	d	d	d	r	d	d	t₁	m	r	m
s	f	s	s	l	s	s	s	l	m	r	r	m	f	m
r	m	r	r	r	d	r	d	r	t	l	t	t	t	d¹
f	s	f	s	f	f	l	t	l	d¹	t	d¹	l	s	l

Singing from dictation may now be proceeded with and will be found an excellent auxiliary to ear training and sight-singing. The teacher may indicate

SINGING FROM DICTATION. by the manual signs which tones are to be sung to *laa*, or may simply name them, thus :—Teacher sings **d s m d** and tells class to sing **m r d**, or any of above phrases which may be desired. In all exercises the pupils who display least natural ability to tell tones by ear should receive special attention and should be encouraged to persevere until they compare favorably with the others. See pages 52 and 101.

PREPARED SONGS.

These will necessarily contain greater difficulties of tune and time, and be of a superior character generally than those prescribed for Div. II, but should be taught by the same methods. See page 106.

VOICE TRAINING.

Tuning exercises in two parts should now be introduced. It is advisable to teach the lower part thoroughly before touching the upper part, as young pupils are invariably inclined to sing the latter, to which the ear is unconsciously attracted more strongly than to the former. The pupils should be divided into two sections, according to the quality of

CLASSIFYING VOICES. the voice. A trained ear will easily distinguish the soprano from the contralto by the quality of the speaking voice, but the ordinary teacher should not attempt to classify voices without first testing each voice in singing from the modulator. This may be done by singing up and down in the key of C. If the best tones are found in the upper-thick register, the voice may be presumed to be contralto ; but if in the lower and upper-thin registers, soprano will be the most suitable part for that particular voice. See page 23. Each part should be practised separately, beginning with the

BEGIN SOFTLY. softest possible tone and endeavoring to have all voices in a part blended as one. Pupils who will persist in singing loudly should be prohibited from singing for a time. The most suitable vowel for elementary tuning of voices is *oo.* When the voices in each part have been fairly well blended, the two parts may be combined, and the vowels *ah, oh, ai* and *ee* introduced individually in the order given.

Examples of Tuning Exercises :—

KEY G.

m	:f	m	:r	m	:—	—	:	
d	:l₁	s₁	:t₁	d	:—	—	:	

Key G.

```
{|d  :r  |m  :f  |m  :r  |d  :—  ||
 |d  :t, |d  :l, |s, :t, |d  :—  ||
```

CHAPTER XIV.

NOTES ON DIVISION IV.

MODULATOR DRILL.

THE first modulator drill for this Division is exactly the same as prescribed for Division III.

In order to conduct two-part exercises successfully it is necessary that the teacher should have a knowledge of the elementary principles of harmony, in order that ungrammatical harmonic progressions may be avoided, and those only introduced which are calculated to produce a pleasing harmonic effect. The most pleasing *intervals are *thirds*, as :—d m ‖r f‖l, d ‖ f l‖s t‖. When *thirds* only are used they become too sweet and insipid, and a new combination is necessary. This is supplied by *sixths*, which are simply inverted thirds, as :—d l‖r t‖m d'‖l, f‖t, s‖. A strong binding effect is produced by the employment of *fifths*, as :—d s‖r l‖f d'‖, or their inversions termed *fourths*, as :—s, d‖l r'‖d f‖. These, how-

| AVOID CONSECUTIVE FIFTHS. |

ever, must be employed with extreme caution, and on no account should

---

* Intervals are calculated from the lower to the higher tone, both being included.

two fifths, as :—‖ s l ‖ t l ‖ r m ‖ be given in suc-
‖ d r ‖ m r ‖ s, l, ‖,
cession.   The effect of such *"consecutive fifths"* is
harsh and unpleasant.   As a rule, four or five thirds
or sixths in succession will be sufficient, and a fourth
or fifth should be added to give variety to the
harmony.   The following will serve to illustrate :—

KEY E♭.

d	m	s	m	r	f	m	f	s	l	f	f	m	f	s	l
d	d	t,	d	t,	t,	d	—	t,	d	r	t,	d	r	m	f

t	t	d'	—	d'	t	l	s	f	l	s	—	l	t	d'	—
f	f	m	—	m	f	f	m	r	f	f	m	r	f	m	—

Before attempting to conduct two part exercises
the teacher should carefully prepare a definite plan
by writing a number of exercises similar to the above
until familiar with the more common harmonic progressions.   A few short and simple exercises only
should be used in the class until pupils have developed
a moderate degree of steadiness in maintaining their
own against another part.

TIME.

In this Division no new divisions of rhythm are
introduced, but those already taught should be thoroughly reviewed until they can be easily sung at sight.

SIGHT-SINGING.

The exercises prescribed for this Division are
intended to enable pupils to sing at sight any ordinary

hymn tune or song of moderate difficulty. When tune and time are combined for the first time, one is certain to receive more attention than the other. Before singing each exercise, the attention should be directed to the difference in length of the notes. Each exercise should be vocalised, after sol-faing not more than three times.

EXERCISE 1. KEY G.

|d :m |r :s |f :—|m :f |s :l |f :r |s :—|m :—}

|f :r |s :—|s :m |l :—|r :s |d :f |m :r |d :—||

EXERCISE 2. KEY D.

|m :d |f :r |s :—|m :—|l :r |m :f |f :—|m :—}

|s :d¹ |f :—|l :d¹ |s :—|m :d |r :s |t₁ :r |d :—||

EXERCISE 3. KEY A.

|d :t₁ |d :s₁ |m₁ :—|f₁ :—|r₁ :s₁ |l₁ :t₁ |l₁ :—|s₁ :—}

|d :m₁ |f₁ :—|r :d |s₁ :—|l₁ :d |m :r |f :t₁ |d :—||

EXERCISE 4. KEY E.

|d :m |r :t₁ |d :f |m :—|l :r |s :d |t :r |s₁ :—}

|d :—|r :—|t₁ :s₁ |d :m |f :s |l :m |f :s |d :—||

EAR EXERCISES.

Exercises containing stepwise progressions should still receive attention. Dictation exercises containing intervals of greater difficulty will prepare for more advanced ear exercises. In conducting the following exercises the teacher will sing the tones of the DOH chord, then *name* the tones to be sol-faed by the class :

m r d s	l f s d	s l t s	d' t l m
r m f l	f m r s	d' t d' s	m f r d
s l f s	d' s l f	s m s r	s l f d
d' s t l	l d' f m	s m d s,	d s, t, d

In the following the teacher will sing on one tone to *laa* while beating time, while the pupils listen, then sing the time-names on one tone :

|d   :d .d |d   :d || |d.d :d |d.d :d ||

|d   :– .d |d   :— || |d   :– .d |d.d :d ||

|d   : |d .d :d || |d.d :d |d   :d .d ||

|d   :– .d |d   :d .d || |d   :d,d.d,d|d   :— ||

|d,d.d,d:d |d .d :d || |d   :d,d.d,d|d   :d .d ||

PREPARED SONG.

The study of two-part songs is usually a more difficult matter than is generally supposed. The upper part is usually more "catching" than the lower, and even when the parts have been thoroughly mastered when sung separately, it frequently happens that the alto voices are unconsciously singing with the soprano. This may be overcome by frequent practice of tuning exercises and modulator drill in two parts. As a rule it is advisable to teach the lower part before the upper, until sufficient skill has been developed to permit of both parts being sung simultaneously.

VOICE TRAINING.

If a reasonable amount of attention has been paid to voice training, pupils should enter this Division with a fair command of voice, an increased compass, and a tone, which if not large in volume, should at least be pure and soft in its quality. A strict outlook should be kept for voices which are apt to be strained particularly among boys, who usually incline to force

> **TRAIN DOWNWARDS.**

the lower-thin register upwards in preference to using the upper-thin. The upper registers can best be cultivated by singing *downwards.* Exercises for this purpose should begin above D¹ which will compel the use of the upper thin The sweetness of this register should be noticed, and pupils directed to carry it down as far as possible *without changing.*

The vowel *oo* is the most congenial to this register and should precede all others.

VOICE EXERCISES FOR UPPER REGISTERS.

Ex. 1. KEYS A, A♭, G, F. ✿

| s :f | m :r | s :f | m :r | s :f | m :r | m:f | m :— ||

Ex. 2. KEYS F, E, E♭, D. ✿

| d¹:t | l :s | d¹:t | l :s | d¹:t | l :s | l :t | d¹ :— ||

Ex. 3. KEYS C, B, B♭, A. ✿

| m¹:f¹ | m¹:r¹ | m¹:f¹ | m¹:r¹ | m¹:f¹ | m¹:r¹ | d¹:t | d¹ ;— ||

For Whole Compass of Voice.

Ex. 4. Keys C, D, E. ✵

$$\left| \text{m} : \text{d} \left| \text{s} : \text{m} \right| \text{f} : \text{l} \left| \text{d}^{\text{l}} : \text{l} \right| \text{s} : \text{t} \left| \text{r}^{\text{l}} : \text{t} \right| \text{d}^{\text{l}} : — | — : — \right\|$$

Ex. 5. Keys C, D.

$$\left| \text{d} . \text{m} : \text{r} . \text{f} \left| \text{m} . \text{s} : \text{f} . \text{l} \right| \text{s} . \text{t} : \text{l} . \text{d}^{\text{l}} \left| \text{t} . \text{r}^{\text{l}} : \widehat{\text{d}} \right. \right\}$$ ✵

$$\left| \text{m}^{\text{l}} . \text{d}^{\text{l}} : \text{r} . \text{t} \left| \text{d}^{\text{l}} . \text{l} : \text{t} . \text{s} \right| \text{l} . \text{f} : \text{s} . \text{m} \left| \text{f} . \text{r} : \text{d} \right. \right\|$$

The above should first be sung to *koo* with neatly detached tones (*staccato*), then smoothly (*legato*) to *oo*, *aa*, *ai*, *ee* and *oh*, breath being taken at the points marked *.

| GYMNASTICS IN BREATHING. | Breathing exercises should be given frequently in connection with the |

above. It is inadvisable to multiply exercises. A few simple gymnastics conducted by a careful, observant teacher, should be sufficient for all practical purposes.

EXERCISE 1st.—Pupils stand erect, take breath by expanding the *lower part of the chest* while the teacher counts four slowly ; retain the breath by keeping the chest expanded for a similar length of time, then let the breath go suddenly. Repeat three or four times.

EXERCISE 2nd.—Inhale by expanding the chest suddenly ; retain the breath for four seconds as above, then sing the vowel *oo* while the teacher counts four. The attention must be concentrated on securing a smooth, steady tone. The period during which the breath is inhaled, or the tone sustained, may gradually be increased to eight seconds ; but it is not advisable to retain the breath beyond four seconds.

PART SECOND.

CHAPTER XV.

SYLLABUS FOR SENIOR DIVISIONS.

IN Part First the three primary steps of the Tonic Sol-fa method only are treated. The subject-matter of the remaining steps is as follows :—

FOURTH STEP.

TUNE.—The standard scale of pitch. Transition to the first sharp and first flat keys. Simple chromatic tones. Musical expression.

TIME.—Quarter-pulse silences. Pulses divided into thirds. Beating of time.

FIFTH STEP.

TUNE.—The minor mode. Transitional modulation.

TIME.—Pulses divided into *sixths, eighths* and *ninths.*

SIXTH STEP.

TUNE.—Transitions of two or more removes. Transitional modulation. Exceptional chromatic progressions.

TIME.—Rare divisions of rhythm.

In pursuance of the plan adopted on page 63, the following syllabus is recommended for use in the senior divisions :

DIVISION V.

MODULATOR.—(a) To sol-fa from Examiner's pointing on the fourth-step modulator, exercises containing transition of one remove in the perfect method. (b) To sing as above, exercises containing the tones **fe** and **ta** in stepwise progression used thus:—**s fe s, d¹ ta l.**

SIGHT-SINGING,—To sol-fa at sight a written or printed exercise including all tones of the Major scale, with **fe** and **ta** as above, but not necessarily containing any divisions of the pulse less than half-pulses.

TIME.—To sing on one tone to time-names and *laa*, exercises containing combinations of quarters and half-pulse tones.

EAR EXERCISES.—To imitate and afterwards name the tones of a simple diatonic phrase of five tones the Examiner may twice sing to *laa*, the tones of the **DOH** chord being first given in each case.

PREPARED SONG.—To sing in two parts, with due expression and fair quality of tone, a school song set to words.

DIVISION VI.

MODULATOR.—(a) To sol-fa from Examiner's pointing, exercises containing transition of one remove and modulation to the relative minor, including the tone **se** used thus, l **se** l. (b) To *vocalize*, from the Examiner's pointing, simple exercises including all tones of the major diatonic scale.

SIGHT-SINGING.—To sol-fa at sight a written or printed test including any tones of the major scale and easy transitions of one remove, indicated by bridge-notes.

TIME.—(a) To sing on one tone to *laa* or time-names, exercises including various combinations of thirds. (b) To sing as above, exercises in quick six-pulse measure.

EAR EXERCISES.—To imitate and afterwards name the tones of a simple phrase of five tones, including **fe** or **ta**.

PREPARED SONG.—Same as for Division V.

DIVISION VII.

MODULATOR.—(a) To sol-fa from Examiner's pointing exercises containing transitions of two removes. (b) To *vocalize* as above, exercises containing easy transitions of *one* remove in the perfect and imperfect methods.

SIGHT-SINGING.—(a) To sol-fa at sight a written or printed test of moderate difficulty, including transitions of one remove indicated by bridge-notes. (b) To sol-fa as above a test including modulation to the relative minor with the tone se used thus, l se l.

TIME.—To sing on one tone to *laa* or time-names, exercises containing any divisions of rhythm previously specified with the addition of quarter-pulse silences.

EAR EXERCISES.—To write in correct *time* and *tune* a phrase of four measures, including whole pulse tones and continuations, but no divided pulses, the Examiner singing the **DOH** chord and indicating the rate of movement by beating one complete measure prior to singing the test.

PREPARED SONG.—To include transition of one remove, and divided pulses, sung to words with a fair command of voice, expression and clear articulation.

DIVISION VIII.

MODULATOR.—(a) To sol-fa from Examiner's pointing exercises containing transitions of two and three removes, and phrases in the minor mode, including the tones ba and se. (b) To sol-fa as above, exercises containing any chromatic tones in stepwise progression, thus:—m re m, s la s, r ma r.

SIGHT-SINGING.—(a) To sol-fa at sight an easy test including transition of one remove indicated by bridge-notes, and modulations to the relative minor, including the tones ba and se in stepwise progression. (b) To *vocalise* at sight an easy test including transition of one remove.

TIME.—To sing on one tone to *laa* or time-names exercises of moderate difficulty, including any divisions of rhythm previously specified, with the addition of simple syncopations.

EAR EXERCISES.—To write in correct time and tune a phrase of four measures containing half-pulses and the tones **fe** and **ta**, the examiner first indicating the rate of movement and giving the tones of the **DOH** chord.

In order that each topic may be more clearly understood, a separate chapter is devoted to the discussion of each individually. The methods of teaching any one topic are identical in all classes.

CHAPTER XVI.

TRANSITION.

(a passage leading from one theme to another OR a temporary modulation)

IN order to clearly understand transition, it is necessary that the standard scale of pitch should first be studied. The Tonic Sol-fa notation makes no attempt at express-ing absolute pitch other than intimating the key in which a piece of music is written. This is done by means of the first seven letters of the alphabet. The scale of C has been adopted by musicians as the standard by which the pitch of all other scales is governed. By referring to the annexed diagram it will be noticed that the intervals of this scale correspond exactly with those of the third step modulator. Musicians have not yet

C'—d'
B —t
b   ♯
A —l
b   ♯
G —s
b   ♯
F —f
E —m
b   ♯
D —r
C—d

absolute pitch = the fixed position of a sound as determined by the number of vibrations which produce it eg C4 C5 D♭

Relative pitch = is the position a sound holds with referance to another sound ie higher or lower - as in movable 'do' - in Tonic Sol-Fa agreed upon any definite standard, but the majority favour 256 vibrations as the standard for Middle C.

PITCHING THE KEY.

In teaching, it is advisable to use an ordinary modulator (third step) suspended by a cord of sufficient length to permit of its being raised or lowered to any desired position. The seven letters being written on the blackboard on a line with the corresponding notes of the modulator will illustrate the scale of *absolute* pitch, while the movable modulator will illustrate the scale of *relative* pitch, with its movable **doh**.   The lesson may be illustrated by referring to the standard of weights and measures, by which all others are measured.   In pitching the key the modulator should be moved until **d** is opposite the letter which represents the required key.   Then take the sound of C¹ from the tuning-fork or other instrument, and sing downwards to the letter required, and sing **doh** on exactly the same pitch.   The keys most commonly used may be readily pitched by singing the note which is on the same pitch as C, and then downwards to **d**, thus :— To pitch G : move the modulator until **d** is opposite G.   **Fah** will now be opposite C ; sound C, call it **fah**, and sing **f m r d**.   The **d** will then indicate the key of G.

We have hitherto changed key frequently in singing different exercises, but have not as yet changed key within any one exercise or tune.   When this takes place it is called Transition.   It serves to add increased interest to a musical composition by introducing

FOURTH STEP
MODULATOR.

d¹		f¹		
t		m¹		l
			re¹	se
l		r¹		s
se	ra¹		de¹	ba
s		DOH¹		f
ba		TE		m
f	ta		le	
m		LAH		r
	la		se	
r		SOH		d
			bah fe	t₁
d		FAH		
t₁		ME		l₁
	ma		re	se₁
l₁		RAY		s₁
se₁	ra		de	ba₁
s₁		DOH		f₁
ba₁		t₁		m₁
f₁	ta₁			
m₁		l₁		r₁
		se₁		
r₁		s₁		d₁
		ba₁	fe₁	t₂
d₁		f₁		
t₂		m₁		l₂

variety and freshness. Transition in some form is used in about ninety per cent. of the tunes in common use. The commonest of all transitions is that in which **soh** of the old key becomes **doh** of the new key. **Soh** being technically termed the Dominant of the scale, a transition, in which **soh** becomes the key-tone, is called a " Dominant Transition." When in transition **fah** of the old key becomes **doh** of the new key, this is called a " Sub-dominant Transition," as **fah** is known as the Sub-dominant of the scale. In comparing the tones of the old and new keys in either of the above transitions, it will be observed that only one note is altered, viz., in one **fah** is sharpened to make **te**, while in the other **te** is flattened to make **fah**. No transition can be made without the displacement of at least one tone. When only one tone is thus displaced, we have the form of transition which is most easily sung, the difficulty increasing in proportion to the number of tones which are of necessity displaced. Before introducing the subject of transition, it is necessary that the construction of the scale be clearly understood in order that a proper conception may be formed of the real nature of a " change of key."

FIRST LESSON ON TRANSITION.

Write on blackboard an ordinary third step modulator with short horizontal lines opposite each note. Direct attention to the lines as indicating the intervals between the tones of the scale. Introduce the subject by ear exercises in which the expectant, leading effect of **te** is contrasted with the firm, restful effect of **doh.**

d¹ —
t —
l —
s —
f —
m —
r —
d —
t¹ —

Teacher.—(Gives key-tone, then sings to *laa* **d r d t**₁.) Can you tell me the names of those four tones?

Class.—**d r d t**₁.

Teacher.—Quite right. Can you describe the effect just produced by ending on **te**? Listen once more and try. (Repeats the phrase.)

Class.—It is restless. It is unfinished. It expects **doh** to finish it.

Teacher.—Now let us compare it with an ending on **doh.** (Sings **d r d t**₁— **d**, pausing on **t**₁ to intensify its expectant effect.) How did that sound?

Class.—It seemed more finished. It was restful.

Teacher.—Listen again and tell me what tones you hear. (Sings **s l s fe**— **s**, which is simply the previous phrase repeated a fifth higher.)

Class.—It is **d¹ r¹ d¹ t d¹. s l s f s.**

Teacher.—A number seem to think it was the same phrase repeated an octave higher, I will sing it as such. (Sings **d¹ r¹ d¹ t d¹**). Is that the same as before?

Class.—No; it is too high.

Teacher.—If the phrase is not an octave higher than the first, we must try to find out what it is. (Repeats s l s fe s.)

Class.—It is like the first phrase. It is s l s f s.

Teacher.—You do not seem to be able to agree about it yet, still you are both partly correct. Let us take one tone at a time and perhaps we will succeed better. (Sings one tone at a time, eliciting correct answers until fe is reached.) Some say the fourth tone is fah. I will sing fah this time. (Sings s l s f s.) Is that the same as before?

Class.—No; it is too gloomy. It is too low.

Teacher.—What is the interval between soh and fah?

Class.—A full tone.

Teacher.—And what between d and t₁?

Class.—A semitone.

Teacher.—We find that this fourth tone is below soh, though not quite so low as fah, and you have told me it sounds like te. Let us change soh into doh and sing. (Writes $\frac{r}{d}$ opposite $\frac{l}{s}$ to the right and points while class sing d r d.) You can readily recognise that as being the same as I sang before, but where shall we place t₁?

Class.—A semitone below s.

Teacher.—Quite correct. Now sing both phrases from my pointing. (Points d r d t₁ d sd r d t₁ d while pupils sing.) You will now observe that both phrases are alike, but the latter is in a new key. We will now build the remainder of the new scale. (This is done from pupils' dictation.) You will notice that all the tones are not on the same lines. How many tones are altered?

d¹— f	
t — m	
l — r	
s — d	
f — t₁	
m — l₁	
r — s₁	
d — f₁	
t₁—m₁	
l₁— r₁	BRIDGE-TONES.
s₁— d₁	

Class.—Fah is the only one.

Teacher.—Yes. We find in this change of key only *one* tone which requires to be displaced, all the others remaining on precisely the same pitch as the tones of the old key. Te being the new tone introduced by the transition is termed the *distinguishing tone*. In making the transition we crossed over on soh, but we might have done so on any other tone but fah. The tone on which we cross from any one key to another is termed the *bridge-tone*. We will now practise changing key on various bridge-tones, and I would ask you to make sure that you sing the bridge-tone and the tone opposite, without altering the sound. (Practise as indicated.)

<table>
<tr><td>NOTATION OF
TRANSITION.</td><td>I will now show you how transition is indi-
cated by the notation. We use a small note
for the bridge-note, thus: sd, but you must not</td></tr>
</table>

measure its importance by its size, as it is really the most important note in the transition.

KEY C.

Writes: **d   m   r   d   t₁   d   ˢd   m   r   d   t₁   d**

In singing this you must be as careful of the bridge-tone as when singing from the modulator. (This is practised, a pause being made on the bridge-tone to catch the correct sound of the new key.)

When the key is changed for a few pulses only, it is not considered necessary to alter the tones or use a bridge-note, but simply to substitute a new tone for **fah** on the same pitch as **te** of the new

<table>
<tr><td>THE IMPERFECT
METHOD.</td><td>key. This new tone is called fe. (Writes fe
between s and f on the modulator and practises.)
The method of denoting transition by bridge-</td></tr>
</table>

notes is termed the *perfect method*, and that which substitutes **fe** for **fah** the *imperfect method*.

Exercises in translating from the perfect to the imperfect method, and *vice versa*, should now be frequently employed. The teacher points to the modulator and sings **d t₁ d s₁**. Pupils imitate in the imperfect method by singing **s fe s r**.

s —dˡ	Transition to the first flat key may be
— t	taught by the same process as above. In
f ᵗᵃ	this, **fah** becomes **doh**, and **te** of the
m—l	original key is displaced by **fah** of the new
r — s	key. In the imperfect method the new
d — f	tone is named **ta** (pronounced *taw*). It
t —m	should also be noticed that when a transition
l₁—r	is made to a sharp key, *i.e.* where the dis-
s₁—d	tinguishing tone is formed by *sharpening*

the corresponding tone of the original key, as **f** becoming **fe,** the mental effect of the tune is brightened and intensified. This may be accounted for by the fact that **soh,** the tone of brightness, becomes the foundation tone of the new key, and so adds color to all the others. When the transition is made by *flattening* **te** of the original key, the opposite effect is produced, and the tune becomes depressed and gloomy through the influence of **fah,** which becomes the foundation tone of the new key.

Exercises for modulator and black-board practice :

Stepwise progression, **s fe s.**

IMPERFECT METHOD.

KEYS C TO E.

d m d r s s fe s m f r d t͵ d
m d f r s fe s l s d¹ m r r d
d r f m s fe s m s fe s f r d
s l m f l s fe s m r f t͵ r d
d m r f m s fe s d m f r t͵ d
s m l s fe s l f r s d r t͵ d

Stepwise progression, l ta l, d¹ ta l.

d s m f l d¹ ta l s f l s t d¹
d¹ t d¹ l m f l s l ta l s t d¹
d f r s d¹ ta l s t d¹ m f r d
m r s f l s l ta l d¹ t l s d¹
d¹ t l s d¹ ta l s d¹ s t l t d¹
d m r f m s f l ta l s d¹ t d¹

Fe and **ta** approached by leap :—

Keys E to G.

ᴍ d ᴍ r s l fe s ᴍ f r s l f r d

s ᴍ d r fe s l f r s fe s ᴍ f f ᴍ

d t₁ d s ᴍ l fe s ᴍ fe s f ᴍ r s d

d s₁ r t₁ d ᴍ r fe s d f r d l₁ t₁ d

d r t₁ d s l fe s ᴍ d fe s l r r d

ᴍ r s fe s r d t₁ fe s d ᴍ s f r d

Keys C to E.

d f ᴍ r s d¹ ta l s ta l d¹ s f f ᴍ

ᴍ r f ᴍ s ta l s d¹ f ᴍ r s f t₁ d

d¹ t d¹ s l ta ta l s f ta l s d¹ t d¹

d f ᴍ r s d¹ ta l s d¹ ᴍ f ta l t d¹

PERFECT METHOD.

In denoting transition by the perfect method, the name of the new key, with its distinguishing tone, is always written immediately above the bridge-note.

Transition to First Sharp Key.

Key C.   G.t.   f.C.

d ᴍ r d s l s ˢd ᴍ r d d t₁ d ᵈs ᴍ f r d t₁ d /

Key D.   A.t.   f.D.

d t₁ d ᴍ r r s ˡr d t₁ d l₁ s₁ d ᵈs l f ᴍ f r d

Key G.   D.t.   f.G.

d s₁ l₁ t₁ d ᴍ r ʳs d t₁ d ᴍ r s ˢr ᴍ f ᴍ r s d

Key B♭.   F.t.   f.B♭.

d s₁ ᴍ₁ s₁ l₁ f₁ s₁ ᵐ₁l₁ s₁ d r t₁ l₁ s₁ ˢ₁r₁ s₁ f₁ ᴍ₁ l₁ t₁ d

Key A♭.   E♭.t.   f. A♭.

d t₁ d s₁ d ᴍ r ʳs ᴍ f r t₁ d s ˡᴍ ᴍ f r d t₁ d

Key F.   C.t.   f.F.

ᴍ d s ᴍ r f ᴍ ˡr¹ d¹ t d¹ l t d¹ ᵈs ᴍ l f ᴍ r d

Transition to First Flat Key.

Key A.   f.D.   A.t.

d m r d f r m ᵐt· d¹ l f r r s ˢd t, d s, l, t, d

Key C.   f.F.   C.t.

s m l s f f m ᶠd m s f m f m ʳs m f s t t d¹

Key F.   f.B♭   F.t.

d t, d s l f s ˡm f m r s f m ᵐl s f r s t, d

Key G.   f.C.   G.t.

m s r f t, r d ʳl s d¹ m f f m ʳs, d t, r f t, d

During the earlier lessons in transition it is necesary to make a slight pause at the bridge-tone until the effect of the tones of the new key can be anticipated. The simplicity of the Tonic Sol-fa notation of transition is somewhat misleading. It may be imagined that when the names of the tones in the new key are so clearly indicated there can be no difficulty

CAUSE OF DIFFICULTY IN TRANSITION.

experienced in singing them correctly, but in practice this is found to be far from the case. However simple the notation may be, the fact still remains that it is with the thing itself that the difficulty lies, and this cannot be overcome without the exercise of a definite mental exertion. Whenever the key is changed the mental effect of every tone of the scale is also changed, and during the first few pulses of the transition it is somewhat uncertain, as each scale is struggling for supremacy, the old being already established in the mind, and the new endeavoring to displace it and become supreme. The following will serve to illustrate what takes place in the simplest of all transitions, viz., from Tonic to Dominant—or to the first sharp key :—

Firm	**d**ᴵ	becomes	Gloomy	**f.**
Piercing	**t**	"	Calm	**m.**
Plaintive	**l**	"	Rousing	**r.**
Bright	**s**	"	Firm	**d.**
Gloomy	**f**	is supplanted by	Piercing	**t**ₗ.
Calm	**m**	becomes	Plaintive	**l**ₗ.
Rousing	**r**	"	Bright	**s**ₗ.

If care is necessary in singing transitions of one remove only, greater care is required when more remote transitions are being dealt with. When two tones of the original key are displaced, the transition is termed a transition of two removes; when three tones are displaced, three removes, and so on, the number of removes being indicated

REMOVES.

by the number of tones which are displaced. The difficulty of singing the transition increases in proportion to the number of removes by which the transition is made. A common error is to suppose that a transition of one remove necessarily implies that the transition is made from C to G. On the contrary, transitions are calculated from *any* key, thus,—from D to A would be one *sharp* remove, from D to E two *sharp* removes, and from D to B three *sharp* removes, and *vice versa*, as from B to D would be three *flat* removes. When the distinguishing tone is formed by sharpening—*i.e.* raising—the corresponding tone of the original key, the transition is said to be to a sharp key, and when by flattening —*i.e* lowering—it is said to be to a flat key. In the Extended Modulator the sharp keys are placed to the right, and the flat keys to the left. For convenience of reference the key signatures of the staff notation with the scale of absolute pitch are added.

In teaching it is not advisable to display the complete modulator until each individual transition has been studied. A much clearer idea of the facts of a new transition can be conveyed by building up, from pupils' dictation, the new scale side by side with the old. By this method pupils are enabled to investigate for themselves, and the distinguishing tones of the new key with the corresponding number of altered tones are readily discovered. When this has been done the connection between the modulator and the notation may be demonstrated by the teacher pointing short phrases on the modulator, and requiring the pupils to write them on the blackboard, using bridge-notes at the proper places. The following will serve for this purpose :—

d	s	m	d	ᵐl₁	t₁	d
s	m	f	r	ˢd	t₁	d
d	m	r	s	ᵈ'ˢ	f	m
s	d'	t	l	ʳs₁	t₁	d
d	s	f	l	ˢr	f	m

The process may be reversed with advantage, the teacher writing the exercises on the board and requiring the pupils to point them on the modulator.

THE EXTENDED MODULATOR.

Doh=D♭ A♭ E♭ B♭ F   C   G D A E B

Lah=B♭ F C G D   A   E B F♯ C♯ G♯

Db	Ab	Eb	Bb	F	C (pitch)	C (Doh)	G (pitch)	G	D	A	E	B
m¹	l	r¹	s	d¹	F¹	f¹	F¹			se		bɒ
se			ba	t	E¹	m¹	E¹ ♯	l	r¹	s	d¹	f
r¹	s	d¹	f	♭			D¹ ♯	se	ba	t	m	
	ba	t	m	l	D¹	r¹	D¹ ♯	ba	t	m	l	ɣ
d¹	f			se	♭						se	
t	m	l	r	s	C¹	DOH¹	C¹	f				
		se		ba	B	TE	B	m	l	r	s	d
l	r	s	d	f	♭ ta	LAH... le	♯		se		ba	t₁
se		ba	t₁	m	A	LAH	A	r	s	d	f	
s	d	f		♭ la	se	SOH	♯		ba	t₁	m	l₁
ba	t₁	m	l₁	r	G	SOH	G	d	f			se₁
f		se₁		♭	ba	FAH	fe ♯	t₁	m	l₁	r	s₁
m	l₁	r	s₁	d	F	FAH	F		se₁		ba₁	
	se₁		ba₁	t₁	E	ME	E	l₁	r	s₁	d	f₁
r	s₁	d	f₁	♭ ma		RAY... re	♯ se₁		ba₁	t₁	m₁	
	ba₁	t₁	m₁	l₁	D	RAY	D	s₁	d	f₁		
d	f₁		se₁	♭ ra	de	DOH	♯	ba₁	t₁	m₁	l₁	ɣ₁
t₁	m₁	l₁	r₁	s₁	C	DOH	C	f₁			se₁	
		se₁	ba₁	B₁		t₁	B₁	m₁	l₁	r₁	s₁	d₁

Exercise for modulator and blackboard practice :

TWO SHARP REMOVES.

Key C.   D.t.m.   d.f.C.

d ᵐ r d f ᵐ r ʳd t₁ d ᵐ f r s ˢl s f ᵐ f ʀ d

Key G.   A.t.m.   f.d.G.

d t₁ d s l f s ˢf ᵐ f r d r t₁ ᵈr ᵐ f r d t₁ d

Key B♭.   C.t.m.   f.d.B♭.

d s₁ l₁ r t₁ r s₁ ˡₛs l t dˡ f ᵐ r ʳm ₁r₁ f₁ l₁ s₁ t₁ d

Key F.   G.t.m.   d.f.F.

d ᵐ f r s d f ᵐr d t₁ d ᵐ r s ˡt l s r f t₁ d

TWO FLAT REMOVES.

Key C.   d.f.B♭   C.t.m.

s ᵐ l r f ᵐ l ˡt₁ d s₁ ᵐ₁ f₁ l₁ r₁ ᵐ₁r ᵐ f r d t₁ d

Key A.   d.f.G.   A.t.m.

d t₁ d s₁ l₁ f₁ d ᵈr ᵐ f r t₁ r s₁ ˢ₁f₁ ᵐ₁ r₁ s₁ t₁ r d

Key E♭   d.f.D♭.   E♭.t.m.

d ᵐ f l r t₁ d ʳm r f ᵐ d r t₁ ᵗ₁l₁ t₁ d ᵐ r s d

CHAPTER XVII.

THE MINOR MODE.

IN the foregoing chapters we have used only one
mode of treating the tones of the scale, viz., that in
which **doh** is recognized as the fundamental or key
tone, but now other modes fall to be studied and
explained. The ear is never satisfied with a tune
in which it cannot find some prominent tone upon
which to rest as on a centre of gravity. DOH is the

tone most commonly used in this respect, but it is possible to treat any other tone in a similar manner,

| ANCIENT MODES. |

and some of the Ancient Modes have actually done so with a very pleasing effect. However, with the exception of the LAH Mode all others have fallen into disuse, this being considered best adapted to modern ideas of harmony. Modes are termed Major or Minor according to the nature of the chord upon which they are built; thus the DOH chord being Major, *i.e.* having a Major third from the root, with a Minor third above, is termed a Major chord, while the LAH chord having a Minor third from the root with a Major chord above, is

| FOUNDATION CHORDS. |

termed a Minor chord. Practically, then, we have now only two modes in general use, viz. :—

The Major, or DOH Mode, and

The Minor, or LAH Mode.

In teaching the Minor mode, the first matter of importance is to impress the effect of the LAH chord by practising the tones l d m only. If this is dwelt upon sufficiently it will soon be felt that the mental

| ALTERATION OF MENTAL EFFECT. |

effect of the tones is strongly influenced by the effect of **lah**. The sad effect of **lah** will be intensified, and a restful feeling will also be experienced when ending on **lah**; **doh** will lose its strong, reposeful effect, and will be almost as sad as **lah**; **me** will gain in breadth and grandeur without losing its former plaintiveness. The Minor mode is never so easily sung as the Major, even by the best singers ; still, practice will soon establish the new mental effects, and the Minor mode will become comparatively easy.

INTRODUCTORY PHRASES IN THE MINOR MODE.

l₁ d m l   l₁ m d l₁   l m d l₁

l₁ d l₁ m   l₁ d m d l₁   l₁ d l₁ m d l₁

l m d l   l₁ m m d m l₁   l d m d m l₁

When the effect of the Minor mode has been established by the use of the above exercise, the construction of the Minor scale may be studied. The Ancient or Historical form, so called because of its

THE ANCIENT MINOR. employment in old national melodies, consists of the tones of the scale arranged in precisely the same order as in the Major. Many fine specimens of this form still exist, one of the best known being the old Scottish air, "John Anderson, my Jo." Modern harmony, however, requires that the Tonic of any mode should be supplied with a leading note, *i.e.*, a note placed a semitone below the Tonic to which it leads, as $\frac{d}{t_|}$. This is formed by displacing **s** and substituting **se**, which is written a semitone below **l**. This is termed the

THE HARMONIC MINOR. Harmonic Minor, because of its adaptability to the requirements of harmony. In singing, it will be felt that there is an awkward gap between **f** and **se**, being a semitone greater than any other interval of the scale. In order to obviate this difficulty another new tone, named **ba**, (pronounced *bay*), is introduced between **f** and **s**.

> **THE MELODIC MINOR.**

This is termed the Melodic Minor on account of the more pleasing melody formed by the introduction of **ba**.

ANCIENT MINOR.	HARMONIC MINOR.	MELODIC MINOR.
l	l	l
	se	se
s		
		ba
f	f	f
m	m	m
r	r	r
d	d	d
t‖	t‖	t‖
l‖	l‖	l‖

Musical theorists have drawn some fine technical distinctions between the manner in which the various modes are to be sung ascending and descending, but their opinions differ so widely that they would only tend to confuse the inexperienced teacher. The point to be kept in view is not how to sing the whole scale stepwise, but how to sing the tones in *any* order. It will be observed that the difference between the various modes lies between the sixth and seventh tones only. They may be briefly described as follows:

SEVENTHS { **Se** Essential to the Modern Minor.
{ **Soh** Seldom used.

SIXTHS { **Ba** Occasional.
{ **Fah** Essential.

In teaching, it is advisable to build up the Ancient Minor side by side with the Major on the board, showing the fundamental point of difference to be in the interval of a third from the Root, then show the necessity for a leading tone (**se**) and finally for the sharp sixth (**ba**).

d'— l
t —se
s
l —ba
f
s — m

f — r
m
 \\d
r — t₁

d—l₁

In the Melodic Minor the intervals between the four upper tones correspond exactly with the Major, the third being the only interval in which there is any essential difference.

In all exercises in the Minor mode, the tones l and **d** should be frequently introduced, and the Minor chord l₁ **d** m should be given as the key chord before commencing. As **doh** is the key-tone of the Major, so **lah** is the key-tone of the Minor. To prevent confusion in octave marks and the relation of tones in absolute pitch, the name of the Major key is retained and the pitch of **lah** indicated in addition, thus,— Key C, Lah is A ; Key G, Lah is E.

MINOR KEY-SIGNATURE.

Major mode exercises :

FOR MODULATOR AND BLACKBOARD PRACTICE.

KEY F. LAH IS D.

l₁ d t₁ d l₁ d m r m d t₁ r d t₁ l₁

m d l l f r m d l₁ d t₁ m d t₁ l₁

d m l₁ d t₁ r d m l₁ t₁ d r m m l₁

l₁ d m l l m f m l f m r t₁ m l₁

Key D. Lah is B.

l m d r t, m l, t d m l l d' t l

m d l m f l r t d' l f r m m l

d m l m l t l d' l t m r d t, l

l f m r l t m l d' m l d' r' t l

With Essential Seventh (se) in stepwise progression.

Key C. Lah is A.

l d' t l m l se l t d' r' t l se l

d' t l d' l se l m r m f m l se l

m l se l d' t r' t l t m d' l se l

d m l t l se l l d' l f r l se l

Key E. Lah is C♯.

l, d m d l, se, l, d m l t m l se l

m d f m l se l m f r t, m l, se, l,

d t, l, d t, l, se, l, d m l, d l, se, l

l m l d m l se l f r m d l, se, l,

With se approached by leap.

Key G. Lah is E.

d l, se, l, d t, se, l, t, d m r d t, l,

l, d l, m l se l m m se l d r t, l,

l, d t, se, l, d m r d se, l, r m se, l,

m f m l se l f m se l m d t, se, l,

Key A. Lah is F♯.

d t, l, d t, l, se, l, d r t, se, l se, l,

m d r t, d l, t, se, l, f, m, r, m, se, l,

l, d l, m d t, l, se, l, m, se, l, d t, l,

l, m, l, d t, m l, se, l, d t, se, l, d l,

With **ba** and **se** in stepwise progression.

KEY D.   LAH IS B.

l se l m ba se l t d¹ m l se l t l

m l se l d¹ t l se ba se l t m se l

m m ba se l t d¹ l se se ba se l m l

l se ba m ba se l t d¹ l m d¹ t se l

Fah is frequently required in the Minor mode. Like the other tones it is influenced by the effect of the Minor and becomes more solemn than in the Major. It should be frequently contrasted with **ba** in order to establish its mental effect.

Exercises with **fah** and **ba** contrasted :

KEY D.   LAH IS B.

l m d l₁ f — m l m ba se se t l

l d¹ t l se ba m l d¹ l f m r m l₁

d¹ l t m ba se l t d¹ m f r d t₁ l₁

CHAPTER XVIII.

CHROMATIC TONES.

THE scale, composed of the unaltered tones **d r m f s l t d¹** is termed the Diatonic scale. The term Chromatic is broadly applied to all tones which lie between the tones of the diatonic scale. Chromatics are named from the notes immediately above or below in the diatonic scale for which they are substituted, thus,—**f fe ; s se ; r ra ; d de.** Sharp chromatics are indicated by the vowel *e*, as **de re fe se le ;** and

flat chromatics by the vowel *a* (pronounced *aw*), as
ra ma la ta. All chromatics suggest a change of
key, and as a rule have their model in the distinguishing tones of the key suggested. By comparing the
tones in the various columns of the Extended Modulator it will thus be seen that **fe** is **t** of the first sharp

> **MODEL OF**
> **CHROMATICS.**

remove; **ta** is **f** of first flat remove;
re is **se** of the first sharp remove;
ma is **f** of the second flat remove, etc.; the sharp
chromatics being related to **te** of some *sharp* remove,
and the flat chromatics to **fah** of some *flat* remove.
A knowledge of these facts will aid materially in
teaching chromatics. The time at the disposal of the
ordinary school teacher will not admit of a thorough
investigation of this somewhat complicated subject,
and, unless in cases where the teacher has had special
advantages in musical training, it is not advisable to
attempt to teach difficult chromatic intervals. The
simplest form of approaching and quitting chromatics
is by stepwise progression, as **s fe s, m re m, r ma
r, l ta l. Se** being an essential of the Diatonic
Minor scale is not considered as being chromatic.

All chromatics follow the leading tendency of the

> **LEADING TENDENCY**
> **OF CHROMATICS.**

tones upon which they are modelled,
thus sharp chromatics have an up-
ward inclination like **te**, and flat chromatics a down-
ward inclination like **fah**.

In teaching, the chromatics should be compared
with **fah** or **te**, as the case may be, and their resemblance noted. One chromatic only should be studied
at a time, and its effect established by frequent

repetition. The following method may be applied in teaching all chromatic tones :

THE TEACHER SINGS :	THE PUPILS RESPOND :

```
·d  ᵐ  r  f  dᴵ  ⎞
 s  l  f  ᵐ  l   ⎟
dᴵ  s  ᵐ  d  f   ⎟
ᵐ  s  f  ᵐ  s    ⎬   |ta :— |1  :—
 d  ᵐ  f  r  ᵐ   ⎟
ᵐ  d  s  ᵐ  r    ⎟
 s  l  f  r  d   ⎠
```

By the above means the attention is concentrated on **ta l**, and pupils become familiar with its effect as approached from any tone of the scale. This should be followed by the pupils singing the above or similar exercises, **ta l** being introduced at the close of each.

The sharp chromatics are most easily sung when approached from the tone above, as **ᵐ re ᵐ, t le t, r de r** ; and the flat chromatics from the tone below, as **l ta l, s la s, r ᵐa r.**

Exercises in Chromatic tones :—

KEY D.

```
d  ᵐ  s  ᵐ  r  f  ᵐ  r  ᵐa  r  d  lᵢ  tᵢ  d
s  f  ᵐ  d  r  ᵐar  s  f   ᵐ  d  r  ra  d
ᵐ  l  se l  ᵐ  re ᵐ  d  r   de r  s  tᵢ  d
dᴵ  t  dᴵ ta l  t  dᴵ l  se  l  f  r  ᵐ   d
d  ᵐ  l  se l  t  le t  dᴵ   s  fe f  r   d
d  r  f  ᵐ  s  la s  f  ᵐ   l  la s  f   ᵐ
ᵐ  re ᵐ  f  r  de r  s  l   se l  le t  dᴵ
```

CHAPTER XIX.

TIME.

IF the methods of teaching Time, described in Part I., have been carefully studied, there should not be any serious difficulty encountered in teaching the more intricate divisions of rhythm prescribed for senior divisions.

TAA FE.

The division of the pulse into three-quarters and quarter may be introduced by the method described on page 86. The notation of this rhythm is | ., : ., || the comma remaining as in the last quarter of *ta fa te fe,* and the dot being moved almost close to it. (See page 47.) In singing it is frequently confused with *taa tai.* This may be avoided by comparing one with the other, and showing how **fe** leads up to the pulse which follows, as :—

```
|d .r :m .f |m .r :d  |d .,r:m .,f|m .,r:d   ||
 Taa tai Taa tai Taa tai Taa | Taa fe Taa fe Taa fe Taa.
```

Exercises for *Taa fe* :—

a. ```
|d   :r .,r|m   :r .,r|d   :t,.t, |d   :— ||
```

b. ```
|d .,d:r .r |m .m :r    |d.d :t, .,t,|d    :—   ||
```

c. ```
|d   :r .r |m .,m:r .,r|d   :t,.t, |d   :— ||
```

d. ```
|d    :r .,r|m    :r .,r|d .,d :t,.t, |d    :—   ||
```

e. ```
|d .,d:r |m .m :r .,r|d   :t, .,t,|d   :— ||
```
```

It may be pointed out that the effect of this rhythm is bright and bold, and is frequently employed in martial music.

| TAA TAI TEE. | The division of the pulse into thirds has a smooth, pleasing effect, which contrasts pleasantly with the sharp piquant effect of the previous rhythm. In teaching, it may be illustrated by short phrases, with the accent on the third syllable, as :—

$$|\ \text{Merri-ly}\ \overset{\centerdot}{\text{o}}\ \text{-}\ \text{ver the}|\ \text{lakelet we glide.}\ \|$$

Exercises for *Taa tai tee.*

a.

$$|d\qquad :r,r,r\ |m\qquad :r,r,r\ |d\qquad :t_1,t_1,t_1\ |d\qquad :-\qquad \|$$

b.

$$|d,d,d :r\qquad |m,m,m:r\qquad |d,d,d :t_1,t_1,t_1\ |d\qquad :-\qquad \|$$

c.

$$|d\qquad :r,r,r\ |m,m,m:r\qquad |d\qquad :t_1,t_1,t_1\ |d\qquad :-\qquad \|$$

d.

$$|d,d,d :r,r,r\ |m\qquad :r\qquad |d,d,d :t_1,t_1,t\ |d\qquad :-\qquad \|$$

With *Taa-ai tee.*

a.

$$|d,d,d:m,-,m|s,-,s :d^1\qquad |d^1,d^1,d^1:s,-,s\ |m,-,m:d\qquad \|$$

b.

$$|d,-,d:m\qquad |s,-,s :d^1\qquad |d^1,-,d^1:s\qquad |m,-,m:d\qquad \|$$

c.

$$|d,-,d :m,m,m|s,-,s :d^1\qquad |d^1,-,d^1:s,s,s\ |m,-,m:d\qquad \|$$

d.

$$|d,-,d :m,-,m|s,-,s :d^1\qquad |d^1,-,d^1:s,-,s\ |m,-,m:d\qquad \|$$

With *-aa tai tee.*

a.

|d   :–‚r‚m|r   :–‚m‚f|s   :–‚l‚t |d¹   :–   ‖

b.

|d   :–‚r‚m |r   :–‚m‚f|s   :l‚–‚t |d¹   :–   ‖

c.

|d   :r |–‚m‚f :s |l   :s |–‚l‚t :d¹   ‖

d.

|d   :–‚t₁‚d |r   :–‚d‚r| m   :–‚f‚s |l‚–‚t :d¹   ‖

Quarter-pulse Rests are seldom used in vocal music, but they are valuable as a means of cultivating exactness in singing intricate divisions of rhythm. They may occur at any part of a pulse.

EXAMPLE :—

On 1st quarter, *sa* fa te fe :—

|d   : ‚r.m‚f |s   : .f‚m‚r|d   : ‚d.t‚d|r .t₁ :d   ‖

On 2nd quarter, ta *sa* te fe :—

|d   :r‚ .m‚f |s   :f‚ .m‚r|d   :d‚ .t₁‚d|r .t₁ :d   ‖

On 3rd quarter, ta fa *se* fe :—

|d   :r‚m. ‚f |s   :f‚m. ‚r|d   :d‚t₁. ‚d|r .t₁ :d   ‖

On 4th quarter, ta fa te *se* :—

|d   :r‚m‚f‚ |s   :f‚m‚r‚ |d   :d‚t₁‚d‚ |r .t₁ :d   ‖

In studying the more advanced rhythms, the common divisions of the pulse should not be neglected but should be frequently reviewed and combined with the others in suitable exercises. The Elementary Rhythms, contained in Book II., and Intermediate Rhythms, in Book III. of the "Canadian Music Course," afford an excellent series of exercises for this purpose.

Syncopation is the term applied to rhythm in which the regularity of the accent is interrupted or disturbed, as :—

|d :– .r |– .m :– .d ||
Taa -aa tai -aa tai -aa tai.

The time-name for syncopations is formed in the same manner as for ordinary continuations, viz., by dropping the consonant and retaining the vowel of the time-name that would be used for a note struck on the same part of the pulse, thus :—

|d :d .r |r .m :m .r |r .d :d .t₁ |d :— ||
Taa Taa tai Taa tai Taa tai Taa tai Taa tai Taa aa

Becomes :—

|d :– .r |– .m :– .r |—.d :d .t₁ |d :— ||
Taa aa tai aa tai aa tai| aa tai Taa tai Taa aa

EXERCISES IN SYNCOPATION.

a |d :– .r |– .m :f |s :– .m |– .r :d ||

b. |d :– .t₁ |– .d :– .r |d :r .t₁ |d :— ||

c. |d :– .m |– .s :d¹ |d¹ :– .s |– .m :d ||

d. |d :– .r |– .m :–.r |d :– .m |– .r :d ||

CHAPTER XX.

EAR EXERCISES FOR SENIOR DIVISIONS.

IN introducing Ear Exercises at the commencement of a new session, the work of the previous session

| REVIEWING EAR EXERCISES. |

should be carefully reviewed, in order that the teacher may be enabled to gain a correct estimate of the individual ability of the various pupils. This can easily be accomplished by means of written exercises. Let each pupil be supplied with slips of paper on which to write the names of the tones of at least three exercises, similar to those used in the previous division. If each pupil's name or number be signed to the slips when returned the teacher will be enabled to form a correct estimate of the degree of difficulty which may be safely introduced into the succeeding exercises. The difference between tones approached by leap and those approached by step should be carefully studied and

| LEAPS IN EAR EXERCISES. |

contrasted. Phrases of three tones in stepwise succession, followed by a leap, should be given for this purpose. The pupils should be told to give most attention to the last tone.

s l t r'	f m r s	m f s d'	l s f r
m r d f	r m f l	s f m d	d' t l f
s l s m	f m f l	r m r s	d' t d' f
m f m l	d r d f	s l s d'	m r m d

An interesting exercise may be given by the teacher intimating that the tones of the scale will be sung upwards or downwards, but that one will be omitted. The pupils will listen with interest for the point where the leap is made.

EXAMPLE :—

d   r   m   f   l   t   d¹, or d¹   t   l   s   m   r   d

If any exercise should be found too difficult, it should be analyzed tone by tone. The name of the first tone being discovered, the teacher will add the

| ANALYSIS OF |
| DIFFICULT EXERCISES. |

second, then the third and fourth. Pupils will thus feel that they have mastered the exercise, instead of feeling discouraged by having the answer told by the teacher.

EXERCISES OF FIVE TONES.

d r m r s	m f s l r	f m r s m
l t d¹ s m	f s l f m	r m d r m
s l t d¹ l	l t d¹ l f	s m r f m
d t₁ l₁ d s₁	m f r r d	r m f r d

The tones **fe** and **ta** should be introduced frequently after the lessons on transition have been given, each being treated separately. Exercises in telling on which number **fe** or **ta** is sung are best adapted for the first lessons. The key must be clearly defined by first sol-faing the tones of the DOH chord.

Which is **fe**?

1	2	3	4	5	1	2	3	4	5
d	m	s	fe	s	f	m	r	fe	s
s	fe	s	f	m	s	d¹	l	s	fe
d	m	fe	s	d	f	s	l	fe	s

Which is **ta**?

I	2	3	4	5	I	2	3	4	5
d	m	s	ta	l	d¹	t	d¹	ta	l
s	l	ta	l	s	s	ta	l	s	d¹
f	m	d¹	ta	l	m	f	ta	l	s
d¹	ta	l	t	d¹	d¹	t	l	ta	l

The brightening effect of transition to the first

MENTAL EFFFCT OF FLAT AND SHARP KEYS CONTRASTED. *sharp* key may be contrasted with the depressing effect of transition to the first *flat* key by exercises, in which pupils listen and tell which is used. In this also the key must be clearly defined as above.

Whether is a transition to a sharp or flat key suggested?

m	r	d	m	s	fe	s	d͵	t	d¹	s	l	ta	l
s	l	s	m	d¹	ta	l	d	m	r	s	s	fe	s
f	m	r	d	m	fe	s	d	f	m	s	fe	fe	s
d¹	t	l	ta	l	s	f	s	t	d¹	ta	l	t	d¹

Exercises in writing in correct time and tune should be preceded by exercises in telling how many tones

TUNE AND TIME COMBINED. are one pulse, two pulses, or a half-pulse in length. Short exercises only should be used at first, and each should be sung once to *laa*, to enable pupils to catch the accent of the measure. The form of composition known as the Single Chant furnishes a convenient variety of exercises for this purpose. As they are to be found in every Church Tune-book, a few examples only are necessary. The "reciting tone" usually occupies a complete measure without any definite duration sign, but for our purpose it should be written as a two-pulse note. The double bar is usually placed at the end of each section, but it is unnecessary to do so in writing ear exercises.

KEY G.

|d :— | t₁ :l₁ | s₁ :— || f :— | m :r | d :t₁ | d :— ||

KEY G.

|m :— | s :f | m :— || r :— | f :m | r :r | d :— ||

KEY F.

|s :— | l :l | s :— || s :— | l :s.f | m :r | d :— ||

KEY F.

|d :— | r :m | f :— || f :— | m :r.d | d :t₁ | d :— ||

KEY C.

|d :— | m :s | d¹ :— || d¹ :— | s :m | r :r | d :— ||

KEY G.

|m :— | r :d | f :— || f :— | m :r | l₁ :t₁ | d :— ||

In giving the above, a pause should be made at the end of the first section.

The tones of the LAH chord should be sung as a preface to all exercises in the Minor mode.

l m d¹ t l	l d¹ l se l	m l t se l
d¹ t l se l	l se l f m	m f m se l
m d¹ l t se	m l se t l	l d¹ l t m
m l t se m	d t₁ m d l₁	l₁ f m se₁ l₁

CHAPTER XXI.

THE STAFF NOTATION.

THE objection most frequently urged against the Tonic Sol-fa system by its opponents is that "it prevents pupils from learning the Staff Notation." This objection can be met with an unqualified denial and proved beyond dispute. In England, where the Tonic Sol-fa system has had a fair trial for the past twenty-five years, "it has made more readers of the Staff Notation than all other systems combined." The truth of this statement, made several years ago, has never once been challenged. In the examination for the Elementary Certificate of the Tonic Sol-fa College, the Staff Notation is not required, but in the Intermediate examination there is an *optional* requirement that candidates sing at sight from the Staff Notation. Of those who pass this examination, statistics show that about *eighty per cent. pass in both notations.* The difficulty of teaching the Staff Notation to young children is admitted by the majority of teachers, and all of the so-called improved systems of teaching employ some kind of introductory notation—in some cases numerals, in others, patent character notes, which serve as a medium of instruction until the Staff is introduced. The multiplicity of those systems only tends to prove that there are inherent difficulties connected with the Staff which necessitate a simpler system of notation for elementary instruction. The simplicity of the Tonic Sol-fa Notation has already been alluded to. While sufficient in itself for all practical purposes of vocal music, and furnishing an almost illimitable *repertoire* of choral music, it provides the most successful means of introduction to the Staff Notation. The stage at which the transition from Sol-fa to the Staff should be made, depends largely on the degree of ability attained in the use of the former. For general school purposes we would recommend that the transition be made not earlier than Division V., and better results would be secured by delaying until that has been fully mastered. The two notations should then be studied concurrently, the more difficult steps being first studied by the Tonic Sol-fa system, in one Division, and translated to the Staff in the next. If the *thing* has been thoroughly learnt by the Sol-fa system, the *signs* only require to be learnt when the Staff is reached. This can best be accomplished by written exercises in translating from one notation to the other. In the Tonic Sol-fa method of teaching the Staff Notation, the arrangement of topics is identical with those already described (see pages 9 and 134). Tune and Time are studied separately, and the same educational principles which characterize the methods of the Tonic Sol-fa system are employed in teaching the Staff.

FIRST LESSON IN THE STAFF NOTATION.

Teacher.—What is this ? (Points to **doh** on first step modulator.)
Class.—That is **doh**.

Teacher.—If that is **doh** what do you call this? (Sings **doh**.)

Class.—That is **doh**.

Teacher.—I do not think that both answers can be strictly correct. Is **doh** something that we can hear or simply something that we can see?

Class.—It is something we can hear.

Teacher.—Then your second answer must be correct, and your first is wrong. This (pointing to **doh**) is simply the *sign* for **doh**. Any other signs might have been taken for **doh** and the other tones, but we have taken those which have been found most useful. Suppose we take this desk as the sign for **doh**; this chair, for **me**; and this map for **soh**. Can you sing from a notation of desks, chairs and maps?

Class.—We'll try.

Teacher.—(Points a first step exercise from the articles indicated while pupils sing, and enjoy it.) You sang that very nicely; but as a notation of such articles would be rather awkward to use, we will try something simpler. I will draw lines opposite **d m** and **s**, and you will sing from my pointing as before. (Draws lines as indicated; class singing as directed.) This group of five lines and four

d¹ ——————— spaces is called a staff, and the notation in which
——————— they are used is known as the Staff Notation.
s ——————— We will now move the modulator a little higher.
m ———————
d ——————— (Places **d m s** opposite the three lower spaces.

Pupils sing from pointing as before.) In this exercise we have **d** in a space, where are **m** and **s**?

Class.—They are also in spaces.

Teacher.—Let us place **d** on a line. Where are **m** and **s** now placed?

Class.—They are also on lines.

DOH, ME, SOH, SIMILARLY PLACED.

Teacher.—From this we get our first rule for reading from the Staff, viz.: That **doh me** and **soh** *are similarly placed.*

Exercises in singing the tones **d m s** from the staff with **doh** *in any position* will now be given. It is a mistake to suppose that any one key is simpler than another. The rules given apply irrespective of key.

Teacher.—(Place the modulator as before with **doh** opposite the lower line.) Here we have **d**, **m** and **s** on lines, but where is the octave of **d** placed?

Class.—It is in a space.

Teacher.—Quite right. Notes may be placed either on lines or spaces. In this case we would have **lah** and **t** above **soh**, conse-

> **OCTAVES ARE DIS-
> SIMILARLY PLACED.**

quently **d'** must be in a space. From this we get the second rule, viz.: That Octaves *are dissimilarly placed*. If a note be on a line where must its octave be?

Class.—In a space.

Teacher.—And if a note be in a space where must its octave be?

Class.—On a line.

The octaves of **s** and **m** will now be taught in a similar manner, the above rules being referred to for explanation. Modulator voluntaries similar to those used in first step lessons should now be given, the position of **d** being frequently changed, and pupils required to remember its location throughout each exercise. It is necessary that they become familiar from the outset with the notes in any key. No mention should be made of key signatures, *sharps* or *flats*, until the third step is reached, as this would only tend to confuse.

Singing from notation will next be introduced. A staff of five lines being drawn on the black-board, with a square note to indicate the position of **d**, exercises similar to the following will be sol-faed from the teacher's pointing:

When it becomes necessary to have more than five lines, short lines named *Ledger lines* are added, as :—

The exercises in sight-singing should be followed by exercises in writing translations from the Tonic Sol-fa to the Staff Notation. By using the first step exercises in the "Canadian Music Course," Books I. and III., which are adapted to this purpose, much time may be economised, as it will only be necessary to indicate the numbers of the exercises to be translated.

Time is indicated in the Staff Notation by the shape of the various notes. The notes in common use are as follows :—

Breve.   Whole note.   1/2 note.   1/4 note.   1/8 note.   1/16 note.   1/32 note.

The Breve is now seldom used.

It must be observed that there is no connection

TERMS NOTE AND PULSE.

between the terms *note* and *pulse*. A whole note is never equal to a whole pulse, in fact it never indicates less than two pulses, and frequently is equal to as many as eight pulses.

The *relative values* of the whole, half, and quarter-notes should first be explained. Simple exercises should then be translated from pupils' dictation, and written on the blackboard.

EXAMPLE :—

Write: |d :d |d :— |d :d |d :— ||

Teacher.—In this exercise we will take the half-note to represent the pulse. As there is only one tone indicated, one line will be sufficient. How many pulses have we in the measure ?

Class.—We have two.

Teacher.—Which sign denotes the strong pulse ?

Class.—The upright bar.

Teacher.—We use the same sign for the strong pulse in the Staff Notation, but no sign is given for the medium or weak pulses.

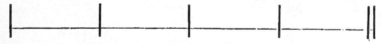

Teacher.—Which note will we take to represent the first d ?

Class.—The half-note.

Teacher.—(Writes half-note in first measure.) And which for the second d ?

Class.—Another half-note.

Teacher.—As the next **d** is two pulses in length we **must use a** different note.   Which shall it be ?

Class.—The whole note.

Teacher.—What reason can you give for taking the whole note ?

Class.—If one pulse is represented by a half-note, a two-pulse tone must have a note that is equal to two half-notes.

Proceeding by this method to build up the remainder of the exercise, it will now appear as,—

The value of the notes is not affected by the stems being turned up or down.   When the notes stand above the middle line, the stems are turned down, and when below, they are turned up.   When placed on the middle line they may be turned in either direction.   The time-names should also be applied to the Staff in teaching time.   The following shows the time-names when the pulse is represented by a half-pulse, quarter-note, and eighth-note respectively :

	Half-note to a pulse.	Quarter-note to a pulse.	Eighth-note to a pulse.
One-pulse note, *TAA*.			
Two-pulse note, *TAA AA*.			
Two half-pulse notes, *Taa tai*.			

A dot placed immediately after a note increases its length by one-half of *its own value*, thus :—

Time signatures are used to denote the number of pulses in a measure.

TIME SIGNATURES.

The upper figure gives the number, and the lower the quality of the notes in the measure.

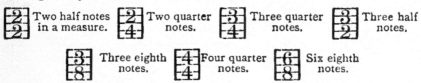

The sign 𝄴 is frequently used to represent four-pulse measure, being unfortunately substituted for $\frac{4}{4}$ and also for $\frac{4}{2}$. The sign 𝄵 is also used to represent two-pulse measure. The time signatures indicated by either 𝄵 or 𝄴 are usually termed *Common Time*.

The following exercises are to be sung on one tone to the time-names, then to *laa* :—

QUARTER-NOTE TO A PULSE.

FOUR-PULSE MEASURE.

HALF-NOTE TO A PULSE.

HALF-PULSES.

taa   taa   taa tai taa   taa   taa tai taa tai taa   taa-aa-aa-aa.

TUNE AND TIME COMBINED.

WITH HALF-PULSES.

SECOND STEP.

Before introducing the tones of the Second Step, the tones of the DOH chord should be thoroughly practised in every available position on the staff.

POSITIONS OF TE AND RAY. **Ray** will be easily recognized as occupying the next position above **doh,** and **te** the next below. Exercises adapted to this step (see page 92-93) should be sung from pointing on the blank staff of five lines, in various keys. The object of exercises at this stage is not to aid to a *conception* of the tones, this has already been done, but to teach their correct *location* in *any key.*

The necessity of changing the key frequently will be obvious. The position of the key-tone must also be kept before the mind throughout each exercise.

EXERCISES IN TUNE.

The sight-singing exercises on page 95, or the second-step exercises in the "Canadian Music Course," may be translated into the Staff and practised in addition to the above.

| TIME. | The new points to be explained in this step are quarter-pulses, half-pulse |

continuations, and silent pulses. In the Sol-fa Notation rests are indicated by empty spaces, but in the

| RESTS. |

Staff Notation signs of various shapes
are employed for this purpose, each
note having a rest of equal value. A dot placed
immediately after a note increases its length by one-
half. The following table shows the notes with rests
of corresponding value :—

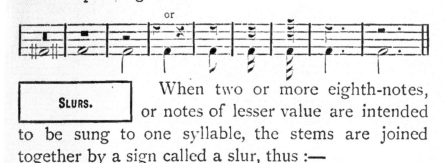

| SLURS. |

When two or more eighth-notes,
or notes of lesser value are intended
to be sung to one syllable, the stems are joined
together by a sign called a slur, thus :—

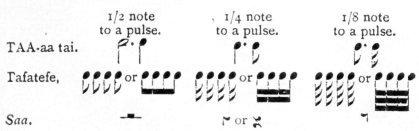

As in Tune, the position of the key-tone has to be
kept in mind, it is equally important that in Time the
Time-Signatures be remembered throughout. The
following shows the notation of the new rhythms
under various conditions :—

	1/2 note to a pulse.	1/4 note to a pulse.	1/8 note to a pulse.
TAA-aa tai.			
Tafatefe,			
Saa.			

The close resemblance betweeen the signs for rests
must be noticed. The whole-note rest is placed *under*

the line, while the half-note rest is placed above the line ; the quarter-note rest is turned to the *right*, and the eighth-note rest to the *left*.

EXERCISES IN TIME.

taa   taa   taa-tai taa   taa   ta - fa - te - fe   taa-aa

THIRD STEP.

In this step **fah** and **lah** are added and the scale is now complete. **Fah** occupies the next position below **soh**, and **lah** the next above. In practice, we have found the most satisfactory method of treating

| TEACHING BY CHORD. |

the complete scale to be that of teaching by Chord. It has already been shown that a Chord consists of a note with its *third* and *fifth*, which is simply two *thirds* in succession. It will be noted that the lines or spaces of the Staff are arranged in *thirds* respectively, consequently the notes of a chord must be *similarly placed* on lines or spaces, and the octaves of either must be *dissimilarly* placed, thus :—If **d m s** be on the lines, **s, m, d,** must be in spaces.   These facts should be clearly understood by the pupils before drilling on the complete scale.   The names of the notes of each chord should now be thoroughly memorized, reading upwards as follows :—**d m s, m s t, s t r', t r' f'.**   All of the above must be *similarly placed* with **doh**, whether it be on lines or spaces.   The chords which are dissimilarly placed with **doh** should now be memorized, thus :—**r f l, f l d', l d' m', d' m' s'.**   This may be done by reading from the modulator at first, but latterly the modulator should be kept out of sight, and pupils trained to name the tones of any chord without any aid whatever, thus :—

TEACHER.	CLASS.
Read the tones of the DOH chord upwards.	d m s
" " FAH " "	f l d'
" " RAY " "	r f l
" " SOH " downwards.	r' t s
" " LAH " "	m' d' l

Exercises in which all notes are on lines, or all on spaces should now be sung from pointing on a blank staff, until the *relative positions* of the notes in any key are thoroughly taught.   These should be followed by sight-singing from the blackboard.   The exercises on page 113 may be translated for this purpose.

CLEFS.

The Staff Notation represents the absolute pitch of notes, by means of signs called clefs. The clefs in general use are three in number, viz.—

G CLEF   F CLEF   C CLEF

The Great Staff is composed of eleven lines, named as follows :—

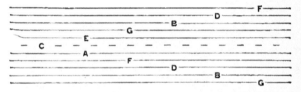

Owing to the difficulty in reading from such a large staff, it has been found necessary to divide it into two parts, with middle C as a ledger line between. The following represents the staff as usually written for vocal music, with the clefs in their proper places. Notice that the fourth line passes through the *centre* of the F clef, and that the G clef *turns* on the second line of the upper section of the staff.

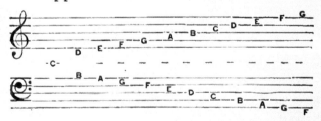

The G and F clefs are always written in the above positions, but the C clef is placed in various positions, to adapt the staff to the compass of different voices and instruments. When placed on the first of a group of five lines it is called the Soprano clef; second line, Mezzo-Soprano clef; third line, Alto clef; and fourth line, Tenor clef.

In the following exercises notice the position of the key-tone in the respective clefs :—

KEY SIGNATURES.

s	C	d¹	C	f
	B	t	B	m
f	B♭			
m	A	l	A	r
r	G	s	G	d
				F♯ t₁
d	F	f	F	
t₁	E	m	E	l₁
l₁	D	r	D	s₁
s₁	C	d	C	f₁

The staff is always understood to be in the key of C, unless marked otherwise. Pupils who have studied transition from the Modulator will understand that, when we wish to write a tune in the key of G, it becomes necessary to sharpen **fah** of the *old* key, in order to have **te** of the *new* key just a *little step* below **doh**. Likewise when we change from the key of C to F we flatten **te**, to have **fah** of the new key just a little step above **me**. (See diagram at side). When a tune has to be written in the key of G, the sharp is placed on the F line, and every note on that line must be sung or played a semitone higher than in the key of C. This will not cause any difficulty to the Sol-fa pupil, who will simply think of the note as **te**.

In the key of F, a flat is placed on the B line, and all notes on that line are sung or played a semitone lower than in the key of C. Pupils will easily recognise that the note on which the flat is placed is **fah**.

By studying the transitions on the Modulator it will readily be seen how the sharps or flats are successively added to form the signatures for the more remote keys. The following table gives the order of the sharp keys on the right, and the flat keys on the left of C, which require no signature :—

TABLE OF KEY SIGNATURES.

Read from centre, either left or right.

RULES FOR FINDING DOH.—The last sharp to the right is **te** ; the last flat to the right is **fah**—or the second last flat is always **doh**.

FOURTH STEP.

In the Staff Notation the key signature is seldom altered when a transition to a new key is made. In this respect it is certainly ambiguous and confusing to the learner, and even the best singers have to pause and study the music before definitely comprehending the nature of the transition. This can only be accomplished by a careful study of the various key signatures, and the manner in which they are affected by the various *accidentals*.

When **fah** is sharpened it becomes **fe,** and when **te** is sharpened it becomes **ta.** A sharp or flat placed immediately before a note is termed an *accidental*.

An accidental affects all notes on the line or space on which it is placed, *within the measure,* unless contradicted by a sign called a *natural* (♮).

If a note has been *raised* a semitone, a natural will *lower* it to its original pitch; if it has been *lowered* a semitone, a natural will *raise* it to its original pitch.

EXERCISES IN TRANSITION.

IMPERFECT METHOD.

BETTER METHOD.

FIFTH STEP.

EXERCISES IN THE MINOR MODE.

Soh sharp is SE, and FAH sharp is BA.

As indicated in the Preface, the exercises are not intended to be sufficient in themselves for all practical purposes, but simply to serve as examples to be imitated by the teacher in preparing the daily music lesson. Space will not permit of a full discussion of the many technicalities of Theory and Notation. Teachers who wish to gain a more complete knowledge of Musical Theory, are recommended to study the undermentioned text books, any of which can be obtained direct from Messrs. Curwen, Warwick Lane, London, E.C., or ordered through local booksellers : "The Staff Notation," price 8d.; "The Staff Notation Primer," price 6d.; "Musical Theory," Books I. and II., price 4d. each. The latter are specially useful. A complete course of exercises and songs for the schoolroom are contained in "The Canadian Music Course," published in three books, specially adapted to the requirements of Canadian Public and High Schools.

MARKS OF EXPRESSION.

NAME.   SIGN.

Mezzo (*metso*), medium.... ....*m.*
Piano (*peeahno*), soft ....*p.*
Forte (*fortay*), loud ....*f.*
Fortissimo, very loud ....*ff.*
Pianissimo, very soft ....*pp.*
Crescendo (*creshendo*), getting louder................*cres.*⟋
Diminuendo (*deemeenooendo*), getting softer..........*dim.*⟍
Decrescendo same as Diminuendo.................*decres.*⟍

Slur, a sign denoting that two or more notes are to be *Staff. Sol-fa.*
sung to one syllable .... ♩♩ d r

Pressure Tone, rapid *cres.* on single tone............<
Sforzando (*sfortzanndo*), rapid *dim.* on single tone
begun loud ....>, or *sf.*
Rapid Swell, like pressure tone ....∧
Da Capo, repeat from the beginning.................*D.C.*
Dal Segno, repeat from the sign....................*D S.* :𝄋:

TEMPO OR SPEED.

I.—SLOW.

ITALIAN TERM.	LITERAL MEANING.
Largo (*lahrgo*)	Broad, large.
Grave (*grahv*).......................	Heavy, grave.
Adagio (*adahgio*)	Slowly.
Lento (*lehnto*).......................	Sluggish, tardy.
Larghetto (*largetto*)	Less slow than Largo.

II.—MEDIUM.

Andante (*andantay*)	Moderate.
Andantino (*andanteeno*)	Less slow than Andante.
Moderato (*modderahto*)...............	Moderate, sober.
Allegretto (*allegretto*)	Diminutive of Allegro.

III.—QUICK.

Allegro (*alleggro*)	Cheerful, brisk.
Vivace (*veevahchay*)	Sprightly, lively.
Vivacissimo	Superlative of vivace.
Presto (*pressto*)	Quick, nimbly.
Prestissimo...........................	Superlative of presto.

IV.—CHANGES WITHIN A PHRASE.

Accelerando	Getting faster.
R.tardando ⎱	Getting slower.
Rallentando ⎰	

APPENDIX.

ROTE SONGS.

We meet again together.

Key F.   A. T. C.

```
{ :s, |d :m |r :d |t, :r |— :m |f :f |m :r |m :—|— }

  1. We| meet a-gain to -| gether,    With | faces bright and | sweet,
  2. A | ring of hap - py | children,  Each | holds anoth-er's | hand,
```

```
{ :s, |d :m |r :d |t, :r |— :m |r :s |fe :l |s :—|— }

  We | gladly greet each | oth-er,    Our | teachers dear we | greet,
  And| thus we stand u-| ni - ted,    A | mer-ry lit - tle | band,
```

```
{ :s |l :s |f :m |r :m |f :s |l :s |f :m |m :r. |— }

  We're| ready    for our |work and play,We're| ready    for our | singing,
  All | things are fair a-|round us now, While| working or while| singing,
```

```
{ :s |l :s |f :m |r :m |f :s |l :s |f :r |r :d |— }

  Our |hands are clean now,| see them, pray, And | hear our voi-ces | ringing,
  Our |eyes are bright with| hap-pi - ness, Our | voi-ces glad are | ringing,
```

```
{ :s, |d :m |r :d |t, :r |— :m |f :f |m :r |m :—|— }

  Then| as we meet to-| gether,    We | cheerful-ly will | say,
  Then| as we meet to-| gether,    We | cheerful-ly will | say,
```

```
{ :s, |d :m |r :d |t, :r |— :m |r :f |t, :r |d :—|— }

  That | we'll be kind and | patient,    That | we'll be good to-| day.
  That | we'll be kind and | patient,    That | we'll be good to-| day.
```

The Honest Toad.

Key G.   A. T. C.

| :s₁ .s₁ | d :d .d | d :t₁ .d | r .r :t₁.(t₁) | d :r |

1. Oh a queer lit- tle chap is the honest old toad, A
2. When win - ter draws near, Master Toad goes to bed, And

| m .m :d .d | f .f :m .m | r :— | — :s₁ .s₁ |

funny old fellow is he,.............. Liv-ing
sleeps just as sound as a top,.............. But when

| d :d .d | r :r .r | m :r .m | f .f :m .r |

un - der the stone by the side of the road, Neath the
May blos-soms fol - - low soft April showers, He comes

| d :t₁ .l₁ | s₁ :t₁ .r | d :— . | — :t₁ .d |

shade of the old wil-low tree.............. He is
out with a skip, jump and hop.............. He

| r :r .r | r :d .r | m :m .m | m :m .m |

dressed all in brown from his toe to his crown, Save his
chan - ges his dress on - ly once I con- fess,— Ev' - ry

| f :f .f | m :d .d | r :— | — :s₁ |

vest that is silv - 'ry white.............. He
spring; and his old worn-out coat.............. With

| d :d .d | r :r .r | m :r .m | f :m .r |

takes a long nap in the heat of the day, And
trou - sers and waist - coat, he rolls in a ball, And

| d :t₁ .l₁ | s₁ :t₁ .r | d :— | — :s₁ |

walks in the cool dew-y night. .... "Raup,
stuffs the whole thing down his throat,............. "Krruk,

THE HONEST TOAD.—CONTINUED.

d	:s₁ .s₁	d	:t₁ .d	r	:t₁ .s₁	d	:d .t₁
yaup," says the frog,		From his		home	in the bog,		But the
krruk," says the frog,		From his		home	in the bog,		But the

l₁	:l₁ .t₁	d	:r .r	s₁	:—	|—	:s₁
toad	he says nev - er a			word ;..............			He
toad	he says nev - er a			word ;..............			He

d	:d .d	r	:r .r	m	:r .m	f	:m .r
tries	to be good,	like the		chil - dren who should			Be
tries	to be good,	like the		chil - dren who should			Be

d	:t₁ .l₁	s₁	:t₁ .r	d	:—	|—	‖
seen,	but	nev-er be		heard..............			
seen,	but	nev-er be		heard..............			

The Summer Rain.

Key E♭   A. T. C.

m .m :m .m	r .m :f	r .r :r .r	m .l :s
1. Patter, patter,	comes the rain,	Tapping at my	window pane,
2. See it coming	down the hill,	In a lit-tle	sparkling rill,

l .t :d¹ .s	m .f :s	l .t :d¹ .f	m .r :d
On the roof and	on the ground,	Patter, patter,	all a - round.
Leaping, laughing	bright and gay,	Pleasant words it	seems to say.

s .f :m .s	l .l :l	l .s :f .l	t .t :t
Patter, patter,	on the street,	Making mus-ic	low and sweet,
Much I love the	gen-tle rain,	Tapping at my	win-dow pane,

d¹ .t,l :s .f	m .f :s	l .t :d¹ .f	m .r :d	‖
To the fields of	waving grain,	Welcome is the	summer rain.	
Mak-ing bright each	tree and flow'r,	In the wood and	garden bower.	

Under the Apple Tree.

Key G. *Beating twice.*　　　　　　　　　　　　A. T. C.

```
|s| :m :m |s| :m :m | m :r :r |r :— :— |
```

1. Under the ap - ple - tree | spreading and thick,
2. On her brown a - pron and | bright drooping head.
3. Gravely she sits with a | se - ri - - ous look,
4. " *Dash*," full of joy in the | bright sum-mer day,
5. Sunshine and soft sum-mer | bree-zes a - stir,

```
|s| :r :r |s| :r :m | r :d :d |d :— :— |
```

Hap-py with on - ly a | pan and a stick,
Showers of pink and white | blos-soms are shed,
Mak-ing be - lieve she's a | real pas - try cook,
Zeal-ous - ly cha - ses the | ro - bins a - way,
While she is bu - sy are | bu - sy with her,

```
|m :s :s |m :s :s | d :t| :d |r :— :— |
```

On the soft grass in the | sha - dow that lies,
Tied to a branch that seems | made just for. that,
Sun - dry brown splash-es on | fore - head and eyes,
Barks at the squir-rels or | snaps at the flies,
Cheeks ro - sy glow - ing and | bright sparkling eyes,

```
|s :m :d |s :m :d | r :m :r |d :— :— |
```

Our lit - tle Fan - ny is | mak-ing mud pies.
Dan-ces and flut - ters her | lit - tle straw hat.
Show that our Fan - ny is | mak-ing mud pies.
All the while Fan - ny is | mak-ing mud pies.
Bring they to Fan - ny while | mak-ing mud pies.

I'm a Little Busy Bee.

Key F.　　　　　　　　　　　　　　　A. T. C.

```
|s| .d :d .m |m .r :r | d .t| :d .m |m .r :— |
```

1. I'm a lit-tle bu-sy bee, | Roaming in the clo-ver,
2. I'm a lit-tle bu-sy bee, | In the mea-dows roaming,

```
|s| .d :d .m |m .r :r | s .r :r .m |r .d :— |
```

Here I go, There I go, | All the mea-dows o - ver.
All the day I'm bright and gay, | Where the flowers are blooming.

Children's Play.

Key, C.   A. T. C.

| d :m.r | d :t.d | r :s₁ | d :— | d :t₁.d | r :d.r |

1. Lit-tle chil - dren in their play, Al - ways kind and
2. Do not vex or teaze a child, Do not make a

| m :s | r :— | s :r | m :m | s :r | m :— |

good should be, Ve - ry care - ful, too, each day,
play-mate sad, But be lov - ing, kind and mild,

| d :t₁.d | r :d.m | r :t₁ | d :— |

Then their sports we love to see.
Love will make each heart feel glad.

Up in the Morning Early.

Key G. C. M. S. *Twice.*   A. T. C.

| :(s₁) | m :r :d | r :d :t₁ | d :— :— | s₁ :— |

1. Up up in the morn - - ing ear - - - - ly,
2. Wake with a glad "Good morn - - - ing,"
3. All through the day He will keep you,

| :s₁ | m :r :d | d :t₁ :d | r :— :— | — :— |

And ear - ly to bed at night,
To sis - ters and bro - - thers dear,
From sin and the temp - - ter's snare,

| :(s₁) | m :r :d | r :d :t₁ | d :— :— | s₁ :— |

That is the way to be heal - - - - thy,
And a thank - ful heart to Je - - - - sus,
So dear child re - mem - ber God sees you,

| :s₁ | s₁ :d :m | r :d :t₁ | d :— :— | — :— |

Hap-py good chil - dren and bright.
Who all night has been so near.
And is pre - sent ev' - - ry - where.

This Way and that Way.

Key A.　C. M. S.　　　　　　　　　　　　　　　　　　　　A. T. C.

d	:r .m	d	:s₁ .(s₁)	d	:t₁ .d	r	:— .(r)

1. This way and | that　way, | Left　foot and | right,
2. Bus - i - ly | work - ing, We | rest　when we | sing,　And
3. When work is | end - ed, And | play - time is | o'er,　Then

r	:d .r	m	:d .(d)	r	:m .r	d	:—

March-ing and | sing - ing With | fa - ces so | bright.
we　are as | hap - py As | birds　on the | wing.
we　has-ten | home-ward To | pa - rents once | more.

The Busy Bee.

Key D.　C. M. S.　　　　　　　　　　　　　　　　　　　　A. T. C.

s .m	:s .m	m .r	:r .(r)	r .r	:d .r	m .s	:— .(s)

1. Tell me, little | bus-y　bee, | Where are you | flying?
2. Pretty child, I | fly a - way, | I'm a　jol-ly | rover,
3. What I gather | is so sweet, My | time it is my | money,　The

s .m	:s .d'	d'.m	:s .(s)	s .r	:r .m	r .d	:—

Are you go - ing | mar-ket-ing, | Pretty playthings | buying?
But I　ga-ther | all the day From | all the flow'rs and | clover.
pretty playthings | I bring home, My | child they're combs of | honey.

Now Good Night.

Key G.　　　　　　　　　　　　　　　　　　　　ADAPTED.

d	:d	s	:m	r.d	:r.m	r	:d	d.d	:d.d	s	:d

1. Now good night, now | all　good　night, | Now to all a kind good
2. Lightly　here day | af - ter　day, | Learning what of good we
3. One will　watch us | while we　sleep, | For He always watch doth

t	:—	—	:	r	:r	s	:m	r.d	:r.m	r	:d

night, | Teachers　dear and | schoolmates too,
may, | All　our　hearts are | free and　light,
keep, | Soon will　dawn the | morn-ing　light,

s.r	:r.m	r	:r	d	:—	—	:

One and all good night to | you.
Sing we now good night, good | night.
Now to all good night, good | night.